BACK IN THE DAY

BAKERY

••••

MADE with LOVE

ALSO BY CHERYL DAY & GRIFFITH DAY

The Back in the Day Bakery Cookbook

BACK IN THE DAY

BAKERY
....
MADE with LOVE

MORE THAN 100 RECIPES
AND MAKE-IT-YOURSELF PROJECTS
TO CREATE AND SHARE

CHERYL DAY & GRIFFITH DAY

ARTISAN

NEW YORK

Library of Congress Cataloging-in-Publication Data

Day, Cheryl.
  Back in the Day Bakery made with love : more than 100 recipes
and make-it-yourself projects to create and share / Cheryl Day and
Griffith Day.
     pages cm
  Includes index.
  ISBN 978-1-57965-556-3
1. Cake. 2. Pies. 3. Baking. 4. Back in the Day Bakery (Savannah, Ga.) I.
Day, Griffith. II. Title.
  TX771.D388 2015
  641.81'5—dc23   2014035874

Design by Michelle Ishay-Cohen

Artisan books are available at special discounts when purchased in
bulk for premiums and sales promotions as well as for fund-raising or
educational use. Special editions or book excerpts also can be created
to specification. For details, contact the Special Sales Director at the
address below, or send an e-mail to specialmarkets@workman.com.

Published by Artisan
A division of Workman Publishing Company, Inc.
225 Varick Street
New York, NY 10014-4381
artisanbooks.com

Published simultaneously in Canada by Thomas Allen & Son, Limited

Printed in China

First printing, February 2015

10 9 8 7 6 5 4 3 2 1

To Peter Workman

His brilliant guidance, kindness, and admiration
for what we do will always be in our hearts.

CONTENTS

THE BEGINNING OF A GREAT DAY

**Biscuits, Muffins,
and More**

EVERYDAY CAKES

**Easy Recipes for
Dressed-Down Treats**

PIE DAY

**Pies, Tarts,
and Crisps**

YOUR DAY-LY BREAD

**Breads, Rolls,
and Crackers**

INTRODUCTION

My husband, Griff, and I bake with love. We own and operate Back in the Day Bakery, in Savannah, Georgia. It's a place where we make Southern American comfort food from time-honored recipes—we strive to create the food folks crave every day.

Running a small bakery and making everything by hand requires personal care and attention to detail, in contrast to the large corporate grocery brands where the baked goods come off a truck with sell-by dates stamped on the packages. Making everything ourselves allows us to be creative with the flavors of the seasons and keeps our menu fresh and new. And baking from scratch gives us an incredible feeling of pride in our craft.

When we opened the bakery in 2002, we set out to create a gathering place that exuded community, comfort, and the love we have for our customers. Being in the food industry is hard work, but it's a great life that gives us a tremendous amount of joy. Food naturally brings people together, and not only do we get to make handcrafted food the old-fashioned way, we get to make new friends every day.

Our bakery has become a beloved neighborhood favorite and a local hangout. Griff and I have made many genuine connections there and nurtured long-lasting friendships over the years. Some children have literally grown up visiting the bakery, and sometimes they even bring me finger paintings that they made in school—I am always honored that they want to share something handmade of their own with me.

And our customers give us the nicest compliments. One day, one of our favorite regulars came into the bakery to buy a box of brownies, cookies, cupcakes, and breakfast pastries and said, "Cheryl, you and Griff have really found your place in the world!" I have never forgotten her words. What she was talking about was not just the fact that we make delicious food, but also the feeling you get when you visit the bakery. We are thankful to have created a gathering place that allows our guests to enjoy what we do daily and to provide an uplifting experience for them too.

Neither Griff nor I started in the food world, but food always made us happy. I learned to bake with my grandmother in Alabama, and her recipes are among my most treasured heirlooms. It's such simple memories of food that connect us to everything that we do.

Griff often says to me, "Why didn't I just go into food from the beginning?" It's funny how life choices can take you in different directions but then bring you to exactly where you should be. In the end, the road traveled makes you more seasoned, and it gives you a greater appreciation once you have realized your goals.

The aim of our bakery is to source the best ingredients, and purchasing local, seasonal ingredients is the key to our food. In fact, both Griff and I were inspired from a very young age to live this way. Both of my parents worked full-time, but somehow they managed to prepare a home-cooked meal almost every night that always included fresh vegetables and other seasonal dishes. They planned ahead and made it a family affair.

It is no secret that my mom gets the credit for giving me the soul of Southern hospitality, and my dad, with his larger-than-life personality, for showing me how to walk into a room and make connections with people in an instant. I often joke with my friends that my mother was the head of the "backyard to table movement" in our family.

When I was growing up in Los Angeles, we had a small garden for the best salad fixings and both a Meyer lemon tree and a plum tree, whose fruit always made their way into pies. My parents also belonged to a food co-op, where we would get big boxes of fresh produce from local farms.

And my dad went to the market every single day. I wish I had realized way back then how much he was teaching me about the benefits of eating seasonally, with the freshest ingredients possible. Even in our hurry-up world, I still think handmade is always better—whether it's what you eat for breakfast or the snack you serve your kids after school—because it allows you to have complete control over your ingredients. I also believe that anything that gets families sitting around the table together again is so much more fulfilling.

In Minneapolis, Griff's mom and dad were the type of people who worked with their hands. Griff tells me stories about his mom's green thumb—she was the one who could bring an African violet back to life, and she filled her yard with flowers and greenery. Virginia, better known as Ginny, was a stay-at-home mom who loved to experiment with recipes and bring her own creations to the table. Griff admired her artistic abilities for sewing and flower arranging and her passion for politics (she was a proud member of the League of Women Voters). And she always had a craft project in the works.

Griff's dad was the guy who worked hard each day to support his family but made an occasional foray into brewing his own beer and enjoyed smoking chickens for his friends. Griff remembers going to the neighborhood butcher with his dad and being able to taste the different varieties of cured meats, from slices of salami to bologna, so he could make his version of a towering "Dagwood sandwich" to enjoy while watching his favorite Saturday morning TV shows. That experience was the inspiration for some of the sandwiches we serve at the bakery today.

People often ask me what it's like to be in business with my husband. I consider myself a lucky girl to be able to work with someone who inspires me every day, but we don't always agree on everything. We have found that it's best to define our own roles clearly: Griff is the master of everything at the bakery. He crafts our savory and sweet menus, guides our business with wisdom, and makes sure that we never rest on our laurels. He moves our business forward and always has a plan for how to do so. I'm all about the fine details of our craft and adding the handmade touches that define the experience of the bakery. I give Griff all the praise for giving me the courage to do what I love every day. We truly are a sweet-and-savory tour de force!

In our first cookbook, *The Back in the Day Bakery Cookbook,* we shared treasured family recipes along with our customers' favorite treats and our method-to-the-magic baking tips. In this book, you'll learn about how we live a handmade life. We share more of our most popular recipes, along with creative details that make our baking not only delicious but fun too. You'll find many food how-tos, including how to build sandwich cookies, how to roll out a piecrust, how to make flavored syrups for your morning pancakes, and more. We give step-by-step techniques for baking our Ciabatta Rolls (page 138), making a tiered celebration cake (see page 164), and decorating sugar cookies (see page 248). The MIY (make-it-yourself) projects—the crafts that give our bakery that handmade touch—show how you can add personal touches in your own home by making cupcake surprise party favors (see page 262); repurposing vintage treasures as lunch boxes (see page 226); putting together a playful marshmallow chandelier (see page 47); and making best-in-show ribbons (see page 123), all just the way we do at the bakery. Paying attention to such creative details makes a party or even a simple meal at home feel special.

American scratch baking is the most approachable style of baking, and carrying on the craft is important to us. We truly believe that connecting with folks one-on-one with food is important, and we want to share the time-honored tradition of baking from the heart. We are thankful to have been able to create a business built on the handmade life. The following pages are filled with recipes and inspirations so that you can live the handmade way too. We hope that you will enjoy the experience as much as we do.

THE CRAFT OF SCRATCH BAKING

There is nothing quite like the satisfaction of bringing smiles to the faces of those enjoying your delicious creations. The process of baking intimidates many folks, but our style of baking is meant to be fun. Once you master a few simple techniques, you're in! It's the small details that make all the difference. Becoming a great baker is accessible to anyone who is willing to learn. Here are our simple but special tricks for turning out incredible baked goods.

Read the Recipe

Always read a recipe from start to finish to make sure that you have a clear understanding of all of the steps. It's a mistake to assume that, for example, because you have made cookies many times you know the method for every single cookie. Think of a recipe as your baking GPS. Be sure that you have the proper tools and that all of your ingredients are at the proper temperature. One of the most common kitchen errors is to start mixing and then discover that you are missing a key ingredient. Yikes!

Another common mistake is to not realize that an ingredient—say, sugar—is added in two separate increments, not all at once. If you don't read the instructions, you are not setting yourself up for success. So, say it with me: "Read the whole recipe first!"

Organize Your Workspace (and Your Mind)

Your most important tool in baking is a clean and organized workspace. Make sure that you have all of your ingredients and tools prepped and ready to go before you start baking. The French term *mise-en-place* means, literally, to "put in place." Measure out the flour and sugar, chop the nuts, and have clean bowls ready. Many baking techniques are time-sensitive—it is disastrous to start mixing only to realize that you needed to get your butter or eggs to room temperature first. Distractions are often the

villains in the kitchen: if you have to stop for a phone call, be sure to make a note of where you left off in the recipe so that you don't find yourself trying to recall whether you added the salt or not. A well-organized kitchen will ensure confidence and success.

Temperature Matters

It is essential to have your ingredients at the temperature called for in the recipe. For example, if your eggs are too cold when you add them to your perfectly creamed butter and sugar, the butter will seize up, deflating the air bubbles that you worked so hard to create, and the batter will resist being completely mixed. If that happens, the air bubbles will not expand during baking and the result will be a flat, dense cake, not one with a light, fluffy, and tender crumb.

The quickest way to get eggs to room temperature is simply to put the whole eggs in a small bowl of hot water and swish them around for 1 to 2 minutes, being careful not to bang their delicate shells against one another. This will bring them gently to room temperature. Don't leave them in the hot water too long, though, or you will begin to cook them.

If a recipe calls for room-temperature butter, that means it is between 65° and 68°F, which is cool but not cold. You can pull the butter out of the refrigerator about an hour before you are going to start (on a super-hot day, 30 minutes will do the trick), or you can cut it into cubes to help speed up the process of bringing it to room temperature. A few visual and tactile clues can also help you to determine whether or not butter is at the proper temperature: you should be able to make an indentation with your finger on the surface of the butter, but the butter should be slightly firm, not hard—and definitely not squishy. If the butter gets too warm, label it with the date and return it to the refrigerator for future use for something that does not require creaming. Start again with fresh butter.

Preheat Your Oven

Start preheating your oven at least 30 minutes before baking to make sure that it has a chance to come to the correct temperature. All ovens are not created equal, and baking temperature can make a big difference in the result. If the oven is too cold when you put a cake in the oven, rising will be inhibited, the batter will melt, and the crumb will be tough. If you put biscuits into a cold oven, they will not rise to their full, flaky potential. Cookies will bake unevenly if started in a cold oven. If the oven is too hot, the results can be even more disastrous. A crust will form on the outside of cake layers and the inside will be underbaked and gooey.

Ovens will cycle on and off during baking, and every time you open the oven door, the temperature will drop slightly. This is why baking times are usually given as a range. If a recipe says to bake for 20 to 25 minutes, check it at the earliest time. And don't worry if your oven takes 5 minutes longer than suggested. Use the visual clues for doneness given with the recipes as well, and always take note of your baking time, which will be helpful the next time you make that recipe.

Know Your Ingredients

It is important to understand the role of each ingredient in the baking process. You can't just skip over steps or substitute ingredients and think it will all work out in the end.

Take the unassuming egg: it performs so many important functions in making baked goods and other desserts, such as custards and soufflés. Eggs leaven, thicken, moisturize, and enhance flavors. Whole eggs, as well as yolks on their own, are great emulsifiers. The lecithin in yolks binds fats and water, which normally resist each other. Eggs also provide structure; when egg whites are whipped to stiff peaks and folded into a batter, for example, the air trapped in the whites expands in the heat of the oven during baking, acting as a leavening agent for light, airy chiffon and other cakes.

Baking soda and baking powder are both leaveners. They create chemical reactions in doughs or batters that release carbon dioxide bubbles that will cause biscuits or cake layers to rise. Baking soda requires the presence of an acid, such as sour cream, buttermilk, molasses, or nonalkalized cocoa powder to activate it. Baking powder does not require the presence of acid; it reacts once it is combined with a liquid, such as milk. Baking powders made with aluminum compounds have a chemical aftertaste, so we use aluminum-free baking powder in all of our recipes.

To Weigh or Not to Weigh— That Is the Question

Baking is a precise science. At the bakery, we measure out pounds and pounds of flour, sugar, butter, and eggs, and using a scale makes for quick work with large amounts and our busy production schedule. However, as self-taught scratch bakers, we use measuring cups at home and when baking in small batches at the bakery. We know that most home bakers don't own a scale. Although we realize the importance of accurate measuring, we know this can be achieved with measuring cups as well. We give instructions for measuring certain ingredients properly so that you will achieve consistent results every time you use one of our recipes.

And use the correct vessel to measure: dry measures for dry ingredients, liquid measures for liquids (see The Baker's Dozen, page 8).

Measuring Dry Ingredients

When you measure flour or sugar, use this no-fail technique (we recommend storing flour, sugar, and other dry ingredients in a canister rather than a sack so that you have plenty of space to dip and scoop): First loosen up or fluff the flour a bit with your measuring cup or a spoon. Scoop the flour or sugar into your measuring cup until it is heaping, then sweep a straight edge, such as the back of a table knife, across the top to level it. Do not tap the cup to settle the contents (brown sugar, though, is usually packed into the cup).

Creaming Butter

To produce the perfect texture in cakes and cookies, you must master the art of creaming butter, which is the foundation of many recipes. Most cookie and cake recipes start with the words "cream the butter and sugar together," often without any explanation of what this actually means. And they fail to tell you that if you don't do this step properly, the results can be disastrous. If your butter is too cold, it will not whip properly; if it is too soft, it will not retain air. The most important factor in creaming butter and sugar is the temperature of the butter. See "Temperature Matters," page 4.

When a recipe calls for creaming butter and sugar, you want to beat the softened butter and the sugar together until the mixture is light in both color and texture; this means air has been incorporated. We've included timing estimates in all the recipes to give you a sense of how long this step will take. Use these estimates as guidelines, but it is also important to learn what the result should look like. Properly creamed butter and sugar will be very yellow (or very light brown if you're using brown sugar) and almost doubled in volume.

Remember that baking is a science. The creaming process aerates the butter; air bubbles are literally forced into the butter mixture. These air bubbles expand during baking, giving your baked goods the texture that you want. Once you master this technique, you will be amazed at what a difference it makes. Your cakes will have a light, delicate crumb and your cookies will be melt-in-your-mouth delicious.

Practice Makes Perfect

My mother always used to say this, and it is certainly true when it comes to baking: even if you mess up every now and then, it's okay. Mistakes may not always be pretty, but they often taste delicious. Whenever you learn a new craft, there will be a learning curve. Take notes and learn from your mistakes. Have fun, and keep smiling along the way, and I promise you will get better every time.

There are many variables to be aware of in baking, but don't let that scare you. One of the things I love most about baking, for example, is the challenge of having to figure things out day after day based on the weather. If it's a hot and humid Savannah day, I know I will have to play some tricks to get my meringues to have perfect peaks. And if it's a really hot day, I may decide not to make chocolates at all and opt for ice cream sammies instead. The more you bake, the more you will learn.

One Last Tip

You will notice that some of our recipes that use an electric mixer tell you to finish mixing a batter or dough by hand to make sure it is completely mixed. This may sound like an unnecessary step, but trust me on this one: there is nothing worse than finding a trail of butter or flour at the very bottom of the bowl when you are scooping out the last bit of batter or dough. This final step can save the day.

THE BAKER'S DOZEN

There are certain tools for scratch baking that any baker should have in the kitchen. If we lived on a desert island (with a kitchen, of course!), these are the twelve tools we would have with us.

1. Stand or Handheld Mixer

Our mothers and grandmothers used a hand mixer for baking; I remember it was a big deal when my mother bought her first stand mixer, a shiny turquoise Hamilton Beach model with all the attachments. It was like my mom had won the lottery, and I benefited from all the yummy treats she made with it.

You can use a hand mixer for most of these recipes, but a stand mixer is one of the best investments you'll make if you're a serious baker. A good stand mixer will allow you to cream butter, whip egg whites, make bread or cookie doughs, and mix delicate cake batters. It will give better volume and consistency to your batters and doughs and make easy work out of long mix times. Our recipes use the paddle attachment, the whisk, and the dough hook, but our new favorite accessory is an all-in-one paddle attachment with a spatula blade. It scrapes the sides of the bowl as it mixes, saving you from having to do it.

2. Measuring Cups and Spoons

Measuring cups and spoons are among those tools so familiar that you never stop to think how important they are. Before measuring spoons, grandma's handwritten recipe would tell you to use a pinch of this and a dash of that to make her lemon pound cake extra special. We can credit Fannie Farmer, the author of *The Boston Cooking School Cookbook*, for inventing measuring cups in 1896. She helped standardize the measuring of ingredients.

Measuring cups fall into two categories: dry and liquid. Dry measuring cups are for flour, sugar, and other such ingredients. Liquid measuring cups are for any liquid. We suggest you have a few sizes of liquid measures: 1 cup, 2 cup, and 4 cup.

Measuring spoons are used to measure small amounts of both dry and wet ingredients. They usually come in a complete set. The most common measurement sizes are ⅛, ¼, ½, and 1 teaspoon and 1 tablespoon.

3. Balloon Whisk

Balloon whisks are used to stir batters, whip meringues and cream, and blend custards. The open design of a balloon whisk makes it handy for mixing and aerating dry ingredients if you don't have a sifter—in fact, sifting is easier with a whisk. Whisks come in many different sizes; having a few will enable you to do many different tasks in the kitchen.

4. Rubber Spatula, Plastic Bowl Scraper, and Metal Bench Scraper

A rubber spatula is your best tool to get every bit of cake batter into the pan (leaving just a little bit behind in the bowl to lick). It also folds beaten egg whites into a batter. A plastic bowl scraper can be used, of course, to scrape out bowls, but we use it to scoop the measured dry ingredients into the mixing bowl. A metal bench scraper is best for dividing bread doughs and for scraping your work surface clean.

5. Knives: Paring, Chef, and Serrated Bread Knife

Invest in good-quality knives, along with a steel and a sharpener to maintain them. A paring knife,

3 to 4 inches long, is best for peeling and slicing fruits and other ingredients. A chef's knife that is 6 to 8 inches in length is a utility knife, best for chopping nuts and dried fruit, among other tasks. A serrated bread knife, 8 to 9 inches long, is great for chopping blocks of chocolate, cutting cakes into layers, and, of course, slicing bread.

6. Mixing Bowls

Mixing bowls come in different sizes and materials, including glass, ceramic, plastic, and stainless steel. We prefer wide heavy-duty stainless steel bowls that make mixing easy. Stainless steel bowls are nonreactive and very durable; a set of six nested bowls from small to large will cover most baking needs. Use glass mixing bowls for melting chocolate and for anything else you want to pop in the microwave to warm.

7. Baking Sheets

All you really need are two 12-by-17-inch heavy-duty rimmed aluminum baking sheets for cookies and one 15-by-10-inch rimmed jelly-roll pan for sheet cakes. The debate about the merits of nonstick, dark, and insulated pans seems endless, but paired with nonstick spray or parchment paper, good heavy-duty baking sheets will outperform all others and will last your lifetime. We speak from experience on this; trust us. You can find these baking sheets, also called sheet pans, at your local restaurant supply store or online.

8. Baking Pans

For cakes, pies, and muffins, you want good-quality, sturdy aluminum pans that provide even heat. Avoid thin, lightweight pans that will allow your baked goods to burn. For bread pans, we suggest investing in heavy stainless steel loaf pans. These pans will allow loaves to develop a good crust all over.

9. Sifter

A sifter is a great tool for mixing and aerating dry ingredients; it will also help break up clumps of ingredients. We specify a sifter (or a fine-mesh sieve) for some of the recipes in this book; at other times, using a whisk to aerate the dry ingredients is enough.

10. Rolling Pin

I have quite a collection of rolling pins, but the one I reach for first is a simple straight, non-tapered, hand-turned wooden rolling pin from Herriott Grace (see Resources, page 293). At 16 inches, it is the perfect size and weight for rolling out biscuits and cookies, doughs, and piecrusts. It is easy to clean—you simply scrape off any dough with a bench scraper and wipe clean with a damp cloth; it needs only an occasional treatment with beeswax salve. A standard 18-inch heavy pin with two handles is nice for rolling out yeasted doughs. I do not recommend marble rolling pins because flour does not stay on them if you dust them before rolling and they tend to drag and stick on the dough. Take good care of your wooden pin, and it will last for generations, becoming a treasured family heirloom.

11. Parchment Paper

I can't say enough about the wonders of parchment paper. It's perfect for lining cookie sheets, cake pans, and brownie pans. It's the best way to create a nonstick surface if you don't want to use a cooking spray.

12. Oven Thermometer

Whenever someone calls us with a baking problem, we always ask, "Do you have an oven thermometer?" All ovens are not the same, and it's important to know where your oven stands when it comes to maintaining temperature. A properly calibrated oven (even a new oven may be off) is essential for cooking and baking. To test your oven, put an oven thermometer in it, turn it to 350°F, and then check to make sure the oven reaches the proper temperature. If the temperature doesn't read true, adjust the oven temperature until the thermometer reads correctly—and then call a professional to calibrate the oven.

Additional Tools

Once you've got the basics covered, here are the other tools we recommend.

BOWLS

3-piece glass set: 1-, 1½-, and 2½-quart
3-piece stainless steel set: 1½-, 3-, and
   5-quart
Large earthenware bread bowl (6-quart or
   larger)

POTS AND PANS AND BAKING PANS

6- to 8-quart heavy-bottomed nonreactive
   stockpot
2- to 3-quart heavy-bottomed nonreactive
   saucepan
Three 9-inch round cake pans
10-cup Bundt pan
9-inch springform pan
9-by-13-by-2-inch baking pan
9-by-9-by-2-inch baking pan
8-by-8-by-2-inch baking pan
Two 12-cup muffin pans
Two 9-by-5-by-3-inch loaf pans
9-inch pie plate
9-inch deep-dish pie plate
Two or more 12-by-17-inch baking sheets
One 10-by-15-inch jelly-roll pan

UTENSILS AND OTHER TOOLS

Apple peeler
Box grater
Candy thermometer
Canvas pastry cloth
Colander
Digital instant-read thermometer
Fine-mesh duster/sugar shaker
Fine-mesh sieve
Heat-resistant spatulas
Heat-resistant spoons
Kitchen blowtorch
Kitchen scale
Kitchen shears
Microplane
Offset metal spatulas: small, medium,
   and large
Oven mitts
Pastry bags and tips
Pastry cutter/blender
Pizza cutter
Plastic dough scraper
Silicone baking mats
Silicone-bristle pastry brush
Stainless steel bench scraper
Stainless steel ice cream scoops: 1-, 2-,
   and 3-ounce
Straight spatulas: small, medium, and large
Strainer
Timer
Whisks
Wire cooling racks

A WELL-STOCKED SPICE RACK

Every baker should have a range of spices and dried herbs. It's the easiest way to add flavor to your recipes, and you can play with combinations to make recipes unique to you. Keep spices and dried herbs in a cool, dark cupboard and date each bottle when you purchase it. Most spices and herbs will lose their potency and flavor after a while. Ground spices and dried herbs will keep for up to 1 year; whole spices will last for several years.

THE BAKING BASICS

Allspice
Cardamom
Cinnamon (ground and sticks)
Cloves (ground)
Cream of tartar
Fine sea salt
Flaky sea salt, such as Jacobsen or Maldon
Ginger (ground)
Lavender (food-grade dried)
Mace
Nutmeg (ground and whole)
Vanilla beans

THE SAVORY MIX

Bay leaves
Black pepper (freshly ground)
Cayenne pepper
Chili powder
Cumin
Dill
Fennel seeds
Five-spice powder
Herbes de Provence
Lovage
Marjoram
Oregano
Paprika
Red pepper flakes
Rosemary
Sage
Tarragon
Thyme
Turmeric

THE BEGINNING OF A GREAT DAY

BISCUITS, MUFFINS, AND MORE

The morning is my favorite time of day—Griff and I are the first to arrive at the bakery, and I still get excited when I put the key in the door, even in the wee hours of the morning. We always frame our baking as one person baking for another, and so that is what we are thinking about as we start to mix our batters and make our doughs. Viewing the process as the two of us making something for one person to enjoy rather than thinking of the hundreds who will be visiting in just a few short hours makes our work much more rewarding.

Griff and I also take great pleasure in knowing that we are a big part of many folks' daily routine. We know that Vivian will call us at exactly 8 A.M. to see what we have made for breakfast, just as she has done every single day since we opened. And the day wouldn't start off right if we didn't see Warren come in for his coffee and biscuit.

Getting ready for our first customers is not always as easy as it looks. We call our crew at the front of the house the "Sugarnauts," and they're attired in denim aprons and vintage headscarves. These are the smiling faces people see when they enter the bakery. And they are the guides for a tour of our cases filled with breads, breakfast pastries, cakes, pies, and an array of other freshly baked treats. They know each one of our regular customers' names and often have their orders ready when they walk through the door. Because our regulars feel right at home, they help themselves to the cream in the fridge for their coffee, and they are likely to tell others who are visiting us for the first time where it is.

We share stories with our team in our daily morning "cuddle" at about 9 A.M. It's a way to connect everyone to everything that happens in the bakery and to make sure that we all stay in tune with one another.

I have discovered that the morning hours can be a magical time of day if you start by allowing yourself a few moments of joy. A little planning goes a long way. You can make our Sweet-Potato-Hash Hand Pies (page 25) or the Honey-Nut Bran Muffin batter (page 24) the night before and then pop these in the oven for a fresh-baked treat to eat on the go. There is nothing quite like Pancakes with Buttered Maple Pecan Syrup (page 42) or Breakfast Bread Pudding (page 44) on Sunday morning to give a day of rest and relaxation a whole new meaning. Don't pour your breakfast out of a box when it is so easy have a handmade breakfast at home.

JAM MUFFINS

*Makes
12 muffins*

Jelly-filled muffins, our take on the doughnut-shop favorite, make our customers almost giddy when they come in for their morning coffee. The muffins are baked, not fried, but just like doughnuts, they are finished with a vanilla-flavored glaze.

3 cups unbleached all-purpose flour

1½ teaspoons baking powder, preferably aluminum-free

1½ teaspoons baking soda

¼ teaspoon fine sea salt

¼ teaspoon ground cardamom

12 tablespoons (1½ sticks) unsalted butter, at room temperature

1½ cups granulated sugar

3 large eggs

2 teaspoons pure vanilla extract

1½ cups sour cream, at room temperature

About ⅓ cup jam (any kind)

FOR THE GLAZE

2 cups confectioners' sugar

3 to 4 tablespoons whole milk

½ teaspoon pure vanilla extract

Position a rack in the middle of the oven and preheat the oven to 350°F. Spray 12 standard muffin cups with nonstick spray or line with paper liners.

In a large mixing bowl, whisk together the flour, baking powder, baking soda, salt, and cardamom. Set aside.

In the bowl of a stand mixer fitted with the paddle attachment (or in a large mixing bowl, using a handheld mixer), cream the butter and sugar together on medium-high speed until light and fluffy, 3 to 5 minutes. Turn the mixer speed down to low and add the eggs one at a time, beating well after each addition and scraping down the sides of the bowl with a rubber spatula as necessary. Add the vanilla and mix until blended.

With the mixer on low, add the flour mixture in thirds, mixing until just combined and scraping down the sides of the bowl as necessary. Add the sour cream and mix until combined, about 1 minute.

Scoop 2 tablespoons of batter into each muffin cup and spread it over the bottom of the cup. Spoon 1 heaping teaspoon of jam into the center of each. Top each one off with another 2 tablespoons of batter, making sure to cover the jam.

Bake for 20 to 25 minutes, until the muffins are golden brown. The tops should be firm to the touch and a toothpick inserted in the center of a muffin should come out clean. Remove from the oven and let cool for about 15 minutes.

continued

Once the muffins are cool to the touch, transfer to a wire rack to cool completely. If they cool completely in the baking pan, condensation will form; removing them from the pans prevents soggy bottoms.

To make the glaze: In a small bowl, mix the confectioners' sugar, milk, and vanilla together.

Generously drizzle the glaze on top of the muffins.

The muffins can be stored in an airtight container for up to 2 days. (Who am I kidding? They never last that long.)

WE ♥ BUTTERMILK

Buttermilk is one of our baking staples. Every self-respecting Southerner (and other scratch bakers and cooks across the land) has good old-fashioned buttermilk chilling in her refrigerator. Why? Because she knows she can use it to make tender biscuits, moist desserts, tangy dressings for slaws and salads, and so much more.

Real, traditional, or genuine buttermilk is a slightly sour, creamy liquid that is a by-product of butter making; it's the liquid left behind after churning butter from cream. Back in the day (yes, pun intended!), farmers would let pitchers of this liquid gold with flecks of butter sit at room temperature so the natural cultures would ferment, sour, and thicken it. Old-timers still drink buttermilk straight, calling it "Grandma's probiotic" because of the many benefits it provides, including healthy bacteria, much like those found in yogurt. Buttermilk is loaded with vitamins like potassium and calcium, and it's low-fat too.

"Real" buttermilk is hard to find these days, but it is making a comeback in farmers' markets and health food stores, thanks to demand from customers and to the local dairy farmers who still make it. Sadly, the stuff on most supermarket shelves is made from low-fat milk by adding cultures to create lactic acid and thickening agents for texture, and it has nothing to do with the butter-making process at all. This kind of buttermilk will work in our recipes in a pinch, but if you can find the good stuff, use it instead.

You can substitute buttermilk in any recipe that calls for sour cream or yogurt. I love it in Old-Fashioned Buttermilk Biscuits (page 35) and Pancakes with Buttered Maple Pecan Syrup (page 42). I also use it in salad dressings and for tenderizing my fried fish or chicken. Give it a try—it just may become one of your cooking staples too.

RASPBERRY CORN MUFFINS

*Makes
12 muffins*

Most people think of corn bread or corn muffins as something to accompany a savory meal, but with the touch of sweetness that plump raspberries bring, they're perfect for breakfast. Swap in the same amount of blueberries (not thawed if frozen) for an easy-peasy variation.

2¾ cups unbleached all-purpose flour
1½ cups yellow cornmeal
2½ teaspoons fine sea salt
1½ teaspoons baking powder, preferably aluminum-free

1½ teaspoons baking soda
2 cups buttermilk
2 large eggs
1½ cups canned creamed corn
¾ cup honey

1 teaspoon pure vanilla extract
8 tablespoons (1 stick) unsalted butter, melted
1½ cups fresh or frozen raspberries
2 tablespoons granulated sugar

Position a rack in the middle of the oven and preheat the oven to 375°F. Spray 12 standard muffin cups with nonstick spray or line with paper liners.

In a large mixing bowl, whisk together the flour, cornmeal, salt, baking powder, and baking soda. Set aside.

In another large bowl, whisk together the buttermilk, eggs, creamed corn, honey, vanilla, and butter. In a small bowl, gently toss the berries with the sugar.

Make a well in the center of the dry ingredients. Pour in the liquid ingredients and mix until combined. Fold in the raspberries, using as few strokes as possible; be careful not to overmix the batter.

With a large ice cream scoop or spoon, scoop the batter into the prepared muffin cups, filling them approximately two-thirds full.

Bake for 10 minutes, then reduce the heat to 350°F and bake for another 20 to 25 minutes, until the muffins are golden brown. The tops should be firm to the touch and a toothpick inserted in the center of a muffin should come out clean. Remove from the oven and let cool for about 10 minutes.

Once the muffins are cool, transfer to a wire rack to cool completely; this prevents soggy bottoms.

The muffins can be stored in an airtight container for up to 2 days. They are great heated up the next day (in a 300°F oven) for breakfast too.

APPLE SPICE MUFFINS WITH WALNUT STREUSEL

*Makes
12 muffins*

Fall is one of my favorite seasons in Savannah, and we love to load up on bushels of apples at our farmers' market. Honeycrisp apples are Griff's apple of choice, and they are perfect for this recipe. You can also use Pink Lady, Granny Smith, or any firm apple with a slightly tart taste. The angostura bitters add an herbal note that complements the flavor of the muffins.

FOR THE STREUSEL

- ½ cup granulated sugar
- ½ cup packed light brown sugar
- ½ teaspoon ground cinnamon
- ½ teaspoon freshly grated nutmeg
- ¼ teaspoon ground cloves
- 2 tablespoons unbleached all-purpose flour
- 2 cups walnuts, finely chopped
- 4 tablespoons unsalted butter, cut into cubes

- 3 apples, preferably Honeycrisp, peeled, cored, and diced (about 3 cups)
- 1 teaspoon fresh lemon juice
- ½ teaspoon angostura bitters (optional)
- ¼ teaspoon coarsely ground black pepper
- 2 cups unbleached all-purpose flour
- 1 cup granulated sugar

- 1 tablespoon baking powder, preferably aluminum-free
- 1 teaspoon fine sea salt
- 2 large eggs
- ¾ cup whole milk
- 8 tablespoons (1 stick) unsalted butter, melted
- ¼ cup canola oil
- 1 teaspoon pure vanilla extract

Position a rack in the middle of the oven and preheat the oven to 375°F. Spray 12 standard muffin cups with nonstick spray or line with paper liners.

To make the streusel: In a small bowl, combine the granulated sugar, brown sugar, cinnamon, nutmeg, cloves, flour, and walnuts. Cut in the butter with a pastry blender until the crumbs are the size of peas. Set aside.

In a medium bowl, toss the apples with the lemon juice, angostura bitters, if using, and pepper. Set aside.

In a large mixing bowl, whisk together the flour, sugar, baking powder, and salt until thoroughly combined. Set aside.

In another bowl, whisk together the eggs, milk, butter, oil, and vanilla. Make a well in the center of the dry ingredients, pour in the liquid ingredients, and mix until just combined. Gently fold in the apple mixture, using as few strokes as possible; don't overmix, or the muffins will be tough.

With a large ice cream scoop or spoon, scoop the batter into the prepared muffin cups, filling them approximately two-thirds full. Sprinkle the tops generously with the streusel.

Bake for 20 to 25 minutes, until the muffins are golden brown. The tops should be firm to the touch and a toothpick inserted in the center of a muffin should come out clean. Remove from the oven and let cool for about 10 minutes.

Once the muffins are cool to the touch, transfer to a wire rack to cool completely; this prevents soggy bottoms. Enjoy warm or at room temperature.

The muffins can be stored in an airtight container for up to 2 days—or go ahead and eat the leftovers for dessert tonight.

FRESH FRUIT TURNOVERS

Makes 8 turnovers

Sweet berries (and cherries, if you like) and our favorite piecrust make a delicious flaky breakfast pastry. Use whatever local fruit is in season for these. You can dice pears, plums, and peaches or grate apples for equally delicious variations.

1 recipe Extra-Flaky
    Piecrust (page 120)

FOR THE FILLING

2 cups mixed fresh
    berries (such as
    sliced strawberries or
    whole blackberries or
    blueberries)

½ cup granulated sugar
¼ teaspoon fine sea salt
2 tablespoons cornstarch
1 teaspoon grated lemon
    zest
4 teaspoons fresh lemon
    juice

2 eggs, lightly beaten with
    a pinch of fine sea salt
    for egg wash

SPECIAL EQUIPMENT

5-inch round cookie cutter

On a floured surface, roll out each disk of dough into a 10-inch square, about ⅛ inch thick. Cut out 4 equal circles from each piece. Place on a baking sheet, cover, and refrigerate until firm.

To prepare the filling: Put the berries in a medium bowl, add the sugar, salt, cornstarch, lemon zest, and lemon juice, and gently toss together until combined. Set aside.

Line a baking sheet with parchment.

Remove the dough from the refrigerator and lightly brush the edges of each circle with the egg wash. Divide the filling among the circles, leaving a ½-inch border around the edges. Gently fold each circle of dough over to make a half circle and press the edges with your fingers to seal; make sure that the filling is not oozing out of the sides. Crimp the edges of each turnover with a fork.

Put the turnovers on the prepared baking sheet and cover with plastic wrap. Refrigerate for 1 hour to set the crusts. Refrigerate the remaining egg wash.

Position a rack in the middle of the oven and preheat the oven to 425°F.

Remove the turnovers from the refrigerator and brush the tops with the egg wash. Using a paring knife, cut 3 small slits in the top of each one for steam vents. Bake for 20 to 25 minutes, until the turnovers are golden and the filling is bubbly. Let cool for 10 minutes, then serve warm.

The turnovers can be stored in an airtight container in the refrigerator for up to 3 days.

HONEY-NUT BRAN MUFFINS

Makes 12 muffins

Some muffins are actually good for you. Here's a healthy version to start your morning. This recipe uses applesauce in the batter to keep the muffins moist; the buttermilk adds some tang and flavor and makes the muffin more tender.

1½ cups unbleached all-purpose flour
1 teaspoon baking powder, preferably aluminum-free
¾ teaspoon ground allspice
¼ teaspoon baking soda
3 cups wheat bran
½ teaspoon fine sea salt
¼ cup applesauce
2 large eggs
1 cup canola oil
⅔ cup packed light brown sugar
¼ cup honey
1½ cups buttermilk
1 teaspoon pure vanilla extract
½ cup golden raisins
½ cup walnuts, finely chopped
Raw sugar for sprinkling

Position a rack in the middle of the oven and preheat the oven to 375°F. Spray 12 standard muffin cups with nonstick spray or line with paper liners.

In a large mixing bowl, whisk together the flour, baking powder, allspice, and baking soda. Stir in the bran and salt. Set aside.

In another large bowl, whisk the applesauce, eggs, canola oil, brown sugar, and honey together until lightened in color and smooth. Whisk in the buttermilk and vanilla. Make a well in the center of the dry ingredients, pour in the liquid ingredients, and mix just until combined. Gently fold in the raisins and walnuts, using as few strokes as possible; be careful not to overmix. Cover the bowl with plastic wrap and refrigerate overnight.

With a large ice cream scoop or spoon, scoop the batter into the prepared muffin cups, filling them approximately two-thirds full. Generously sprinkle the tops with raw sugar.

Bake for 24 to 28 minutes, until the muffins are golden brown. The tops should be firm to the touch and a toothpick inserted in the center of a muffin should come out clean. Remove from the oven and let cool for about 10 minutes.

Once the muffins are cool to the touch, transfer to a wire rack to cool completely; this prevents soggy bottoms. Enjoy warm or at room temperature.

The muffins can be stored in an airtight container for up to 3 days.

SWEET-POTATO-HASH HAND PIES

Makes 10 hand pies

Inspired by our British friends Johdi and Rico, we turned their favorite "bangers and mash" into a savory breakfast hand pie. Bangers and mash is a funny British name for sausage and mashed potatoes (and usually mushy peas). Here the sausage is ground and mixed with diced sweet potato into a hash and stuffed into our flaky piecrust. These can be assembled the day before and baked first thing in the morning.

1 recipe Extra-Flaky Piecrust (page 120)

FOR THE FILLING

½ pound breakfast sausage, casings removed

Fine sea salt and freshly ground black pepper

½ teaspoon rubbed sage (see Tip, page 45)

½ teaspoon dried thyme

¼ teaspoon red pepper flakes

Pinch of freshly grated nutmeg

1½ cups diced (¼-inch pieces) sweet onions

1 tablespoon minced garlic

1 cup diced (¼-inch pieces) peeled sweet potatoes

⅔ cup peeled and diced (¼-inch pieces) apple

1 egg, lightly beaten with a pinch of fine sea salt for egg wash

SPECIAL EQUIPMENT

One 3-inch round cookie cutter

On a lightly floured surface, one at a time, roll out each piece of dough to an ⅛-inch thickness. Using a 3-inch round cookie cutter, cut out 10 circles from each piece (reroll the scraps if necessary to get 20 circles). Place the circles on a baking sheet, cover, and refrigerate while you make the filling.

In a small bowl, combine the sausage, ½ teaspoon salt, ¼ teaspoon black pepper, the sage, thyme, pepper flakes, and nutmeg, mixing with a metal spoon or by hand.

In a large skillet, cook the sausage mixture over medium-high heat, stirring occasionally, until evenly browned, 6 to 8 minutes. Transfer to a medium bowl and set aside. Drain most of the fat from the pan, leaving a little bit to cook the vegetables.

Add the onions to the skillet and cook over medium-high heat until tender, about 6 minutes. Add the garlic and stir for 1 minute. Add the sweet potatoes and apple, stir to distribute the ingredients evenly, and season with salt and pepper to taste. Cook, stirring occasionally, until the ingredients start to take on color, 6 to 10 minutes. Add to the bowl with the sausage and let cool to room temperature.

Line a baking sheet with parchment.

continued

Remove the dough rounds from the refrigerator. Lightly brush the edges of 10 of the rounds with the egg wash. Divide the filling among the circles. Lay the remaining 10 rounds on top, stretching them to cover the filling and to meet the edges of the bottom crusts. Seal the edges with a fork and press the tops slightly to flatten the pies. Place the pies on the prepared baking sheet and refrigerate for 1 hour. Refrigerate the remaining egg wash.

Position a rack in the middle of the oven and preheat the oven to 375°F.

Remove the hand pies from the refrigerator and brush the tops with the egg wash. Using a paring knife, make 2 slits in the top of each hand pie for steam vents.

Bake the hand pies for 25 to 30 minutes, until golden brown, rotating the pan halfway through for even cooking. Let cool for 10 minutes, then serve warm.

Once cooled, the hand pies can be stored in an airtight container in the refrigerator for up to 3 days. They can be reheated in a 350°F oven for 10 to 15 minutes.

CINNAMON WALNUT BREAD

Makes 2 loaves

Griff loves cinnamon swirl bread so much that he had to come up with his own recipe. The trick to getting a perfect cinnamon swirl in the center is to lightly mist the dough with water and then pat the cinnamon filling all over it before rolling it up like a jelly roll. This bread is great for toast.

4 cups unbleached all-purpose flour
¼ cup granulated sugar
½ teaspoon ground cardamom
⅛ teaspoon ground allspice
Pinch of ground cloves
1 teaspoon fine sea salt
1½ teaspoons instant yeast
2 large eggs, at room temperature
4 tablespoons unsalted butter, at room temperature

1 cup whole milk
½ cup dried currants
½ cup walnuts, finely chopped

FOR THE CINNAMON FILLING
½ cup confectioners' sugar
1½ tablespoons ground cinnamon
1 teaspoon pure vanilla extract
¼ teaspoon fine sea salt

1 large egg, lightly beaten with a pinch of fine sea salt for egg wash

SPECIAL EQUIPMENT
Spray mister
Instant-read thermometer

In the bowl of a stand mixer fitted with the dough hook, combine the flour, sugar, spices, salt, and yeast. Turn the mixer on to low speed and add the eggs, butter, and milk, mixing well. Add the currants and walnuts, raise the speed to medium-low, and mix for 6 minutes, or until the dough is smooth.

Scrape the dough onto a lightly floured work surface. Knead a few times to distribute the currants and walnuts evenly and shape into a ball.

Oil a large bowl, put the dough in the bowl, and cover airtight with plastic wrap. Set in a warm place and let the dough rise for 2 hours, or until doubled in size.

To prepare the cinnamon filling: Whisk the confectioners' sugar, cinnamon, vanilla, and salt together in a small bowl.

Lightly spray two 9-by-5-inch bread pans with nonstick spray.

continued

Transfer the risen dough to a lightly floured work surface and divide into 2 equal pieces. Using a rolling pin, gently roll one piece into an 8-by-12-inch rectangle.

Using a spray bottle, lightly mist the dough with water. Sprinkle half of the cinnamon filling evenly over the dough and then press it lightly into the dough. Lightly mist the sugar mixture and, starting from a short side, roll the dough up into a log. Pinch the seam to seal, and put the roll seam side down in one of the prepared bread pans. Repeat the process with the second piece of dough.

Cover each loaf pan with plastic wrap and let the dough rise again in a warm place for 2 hours, or until doubled in size; the loaves should rise about 1 inch above the rims of the pans.

Meanwhile, position a rack in the middle of the oven and preheat the oven to 350°F.

Brush the tops of the loaves with the egg wash. Place the loaves side by side in the oven and bake for 20 minutes. Rotate the pans and bake for an additional 15 to 20 minutes, until the internal temperature reaches 190°F on an instant-read thermometer. The crust should be a deep golden brown. Let cool for 10 to 15 minutes.

Remove the bread from the pans and place on a wire rack to cool completely.

Stored in an airtight container, the cinnamon bread will keep for up to 3 days. To freeze, wrap each loaf in plastic wrap and then aluminum foil; the bread will keep for up to 1 month.

CHOCOLATE BUBBLE LOAF

*Makes
1 loaf*

Bubble Loaf is a pull-apart bread that some people know as Monkey Bread. Our version is made with a yeasted dough. My favorite foods are things you eat with your hands, which means this breakfast bread is right up my alley. It has a delicate buttery crumb and a sweet chocolate filling. Just before serving, it is drizzled with a bright lemon glaze.

2¾ cups unbleached all-purpose flour
¼ cup granulated sugar
1½ teaspoons instant yeast
¾ teaspoon fine sea salt
4 tablespoons unsalted butter, at room temperature
1 large egg yolk
1 cup whole milk, at room temperature

FOR THE CHOCOLATE FILLING
1 cup semisweet chocolate chips, finely chopped, or 6 ounces semisweet chocolate, finely chopped
½ cup granulated sugar
2 teaspoons unsweetened cocoa powder

FOR THE LEMON GLAZE
1 cup confectioners' sugar
1 teaspoon grated lemon zest
2 to 3 tablespoons fresh lemon juice

SPECIAL EQUIPMENT
Instant-read thermometer

In the bowl of a stand mixer fitted with the dough hook, combine the flour, sugar, yeast, and salt. Turn the mixer on to low speed and mix the dry ingredients. Add the butter, egg yolk, and milk, mixing until the ingredients come together. Then mix for another 6 minutes, or until a smooth dough forms.

Scrape the dough onto a lightly floured work surface, knead it a few times, and form it into a ball. Put the dough in an oiled medium bowl and cover airtight with plastic wrap. Allow the dough to rise in a warm place for 2 hours, or until doubled in size.

To make the filling: In a small bowl, mix together the chocolate chips, sugar, and cocoa powder.

Lightly spray a 9-by-5-inch loaf pan with nonstick spray.

Remove the risen dough from the bowl and gently press and shape it into an 8-inch square. Cut the dough into 16 equal pieces. Form each piece into a round ball.

Arrange 8 dough balls in the bottom of the prepared loaf pan. Sprinkle with half of the chocolate filling. Arrange the remaining dough balls on top and sprinkle with the remaining chocolate filling.

continued

Cover the pan loosely with plastic wrap and allow the dough to rise in a warm place for 1 hour, or until doubled in size; it should crest the sides of the pan by about 1 inch.

Meanwhile, position a rack in the middle of the oven and preheat the oven to 325°F.

Put the loaf in the oven and bake for 20 minutes. Rotate the pan and bake for an additional 10 to 15 minutes, until the internal temperature reaches 190°F on an instant-read thermometer. Put the pan on a rack and cool for 10 minutes.

Meanwhile, make the glaze: In a small bowl, stir together the confectioners' sugar, lemon zest, and 2 tablespoons of the lemon juice until smooth; if necessary, thin the glaze with up to 1 tablespoon more lemon juice.

Invert the loaf onto a serving dish and turn right side up. Drizzle the lemon glaze over the loaf and serve warm.

Stored in an airtight container, the bread will keep for up to 3 days. To freeze, wrap in plastic wrap and then aluminum foil; it'll keep for up to 1 month.

OLD-FASHIONED BUTTERMILK BISCUITS

Makes 12 biscuits

In the South, biscuits are treated with the same respect as a fine French croissant. Everyone has a secret family recipe and technique that make the perfect biscuit. Well, here is mine: I gently roll and then fold my biscuit dough. You will see big chunks of butter peeking through the dough, which makes for a very delicate, flaky result. People always say not to overwork your dough, especially when it comes to biscuits. My way of handling the dough will help you avoid that overworking.

I like to turn my biscuits into breakfast sandwiches. Split a warm biscuit and stuff it with a fried egg, candied bacon, grated cheese, or anything you desire. For my favorite egg sandwich recipe, see the Sweet Note. But remember: biscuits are not just for breakfast—they can be enjoyed anytime, all day, at any meal.

2½ cups unbleached self-rising flour, preferably White Lily
¼ teaspoon fine sea salt
¼ teaspoon granulated sugar

8 tablespoons (1 stick) cold unsalted butter, cut into ½-inch cubes
2 tablespoons cold vegetable shortening, cut into ½-inch pieces
1½ to 2 cups buttermilk

4 tablespoons unsalted butter, melted, for brushing

SPECIAL EQUIPMENT
One 3-inch biscuit cutter

Position a rack in the middle of the oven and preheat the oven to 500°F. Line a baking sheet with parchment.

In a large mixing bowl, whisk together the flour, salt, and sugar. Add the cold butter and shortening and, working quickly, cut them in with a pastry blender or by pinching with your fingertips and smearing the butter and shortening into the flour. You should have various-sized pieces of butter, ranging from sandy patches to pea-sized chunks, with some larger bits as well. Be prepared to get messy! I always start out with one messy hand to work the dough and one clean hand to pour in the buttermilk, but before long I have two messy hands and am covered in flour. I pray the phone doesn't ring while I'm making biscuits!

Make a well in the center of the dry ingredients and gradually pour in the 1½ cups of buttermilk, gently mixing with one hand or a rubber spatula until the dough starts to come together into a mass. If the dough seems dry and crumbly, gradually add up to ½ cup more buttermilk. The dough will be very sticky.

Gently turn the dough out onto a floured work surface or pastry cloth. (Remember, I promised you a mess! You can go ahead and wash and dry your hands now.)

Flour a rolling pin and roll the dough out to a ¾-inch-thick rectangle. Gently fold the top third of the dough over the center, and then fold the bottom third up over the center and roll it out again to a ½-inch thickness. Rotate the dough a quarter turn and repeat the process, then repeat one more time. The dough should be smooth, but you should still see small bits of butter peeking through.

Dip the edges of a 3-inch biscuit cutter into flour and begin to punch out the biscuits; do not twist the cutter, as you will seal the layers of dough and the biscuits won't rise as high. Punch out the biscuits as close together as possible, then carefully gather up your scraps, gently roll them out again (there is no need to fold the dough again), and cut out more biscuits.

Arrange the biscuits on the prepared baking sheet, placing them close together so that they barely "kiss" one another. Lightly brush the tops of the biscuits with about half of the melted butter.

Place the biscuits in the oven, immediately reduce the temperature to 450°F, and bake for 18 to 20 minutes, until golden brown. Remove the biscuits from the oven and immediately brush the tops with the remaining melted butter.

Biscuits are best served hot out of the oven, and you will want to sample at least one immediately to give yourself a pat on the back. However, they can be stored in an airtight container for up to 1 day. To reheat, wrap in foil and warm in a 400°F oven for 5 to 8 minutes. You can also freeze any leftover biscuits. There is no need to defrost the biscuits—just wrap them in foil and bake in a 400°F oven for 25 minutes, then open the foil and bake for an additional 5 minutes.

VARIATION: JAM-FILLED BUTTERMILK BISCUITS

Biscuits are the jam! Here's another great way to enjoy our buttermilk biscuits. Roll and cut out the biscuits. Then, press the center of each biscuit with your thumb to make a little indentation. Fill each biscuit with a heaping teaspoon of Raspberry Jam (page 266), Blackberry Lime Jam (page 269), or your favorite jam. Brush with egg wash (1 egg, lightly beaten with a pinch of fine sea salt) and sprinkle the tops with raw sugar. Bake at 450°F for 18 to 20 minutes, until the biscuits are golden and the jam is bubbling. Serve warm.

HOW TO MAKE MY FAVORITE BISCUIT SANDWICH

I've always made biscuits at home, but we only recently starting making them at the bakery on the weekends. When a neighbor from Boys II Men Barbershop told me they tasted "just like Mom's," I took it as a huge compliment. Griff added this delicious cheesy-egg sandwich to our weekend breakfast menu, and it was a hit from day one. *Serves 8*

FOR THE CASSEROLE
1½ tablespoons unsalted butter, melted
2 cups shredded extra-sharp cheddar
   cheese (about 8 ounces)
9 large eggs
1 cup heavy cream
½ teaspoon fine sea salt
½ teaspoon dry mustard
¼ teaspoon rubbed sage (see Tip, page 45)
¼ teaspoon freshly ground black pepper
¼ teaspoon red pepper flakes (optional)

FOR SANDWICHES
8 Old-Fashioned Buttermilk Biscuits (page 35), split
8 slices cooked bacon (optional)

Position a rack in the middle of the oven and preheat the oven to 350°F.

Pour the melted butter into an 8-by-8-inch glass baking dish and spread the butter over the bottom and sides of the dish. Cover the bottom of the dish with the cheese.

In a large bowl, give the eggs a good whisk. Add the cream and whisk again. Add the salt, mustard, sage, pepper, and red pepper flakes, if using, and whisk until combined. Pour the egg mixture over the cheese, making sure it fills in all areas of the dish evenly.

Bake for 25 to 30 minutes, until the top of the casserole poofs up and is golden brown and the center is set.

Cut the casserole into squares and serve warm. (Leave the oven on if making sandwiches.)

To make biscuit sandwiches, fill each biscuit with a square of egg casserole and a slice of bacon, if you're feeling greedy. Wrap each one in foil and bake for 10 minutes.

WALNUT WHEAT BISCONES

Makes 12 biscones

The biscone, a cross between a biscuit and a scone, is a trademark at the bakery. Our revolutionary one-bowl, no-roll technique is a time-saver, and it also results in a tender pastry. This version adds whole wheat flour to the mix to make it a little healthier and give it a nuttier flavor. With brown sugar, walnuts, and a sorghum glaze, the biscone takes on a warm caramely flavor that is great for breakfast in the cooler months. I have included several variations, but I bet you will come up with new creations of your own.

2¼ cups unbleached all-purpose flour

¾ cup whole wheat flour

¼ cup packed light brown sugar

2 tablespoons baking powder, preferably aluminum-free

¾ teaspoon fine sea salt

¼ teaspoon ground cinnamon

½ pound (2 sticks) cold unsalted butter, cut into ½-inch cubes

1 cup walnuts, toasted and chopped

2 cups buttermilk, or more as needed

¼ cup whole milk for brushing

FOR THE GLAZE

¾ cup confectioners' sugar

1 tablespoon sorghum or maple syrup

1 tablespoon whole milk

1 teaspoon pure vanilla extract

Position a rack in the middle of the oven and preheat the oven to 375°F. Line a baking sheet with parchment.

In a large mixing bowl, combine both flours, the brown sugar, baking powder, salt, and cinnamon and whisk until completely blended. Add the butter chunks and, working quickly, cut them in with a pastry blender. You should have various-sized pieces of butter, ranging from sandy patches to pea-sized chunks, with some larger bits as well. Add the walnuts and toss to distribute them evenly.

Gradually pour in the buttermilk, gently folding the ingredients together until you have a soft dough and there are no bits of flour in the bottom of the bowl; you should still see lumps of butter in the dough. The dough should be moist and slightly sticky; if it seems dry, add a little more buttermilk.

With lightly floured hands, gently pat the dough down into a round in the bowl. Dust the top of the dough lightly with flour. Using a large ice cream scoop or spoon, scoop mounds of dough onto the prepared baking sheet, arranging them about 2 inches apart so that the biscones have room to rise and puff up.

With lightly floured hands, gently tap down the tops of the biscones with your palms. Brush the tops of the biscones liberally with the whole milk.

Bake for 20 to 25 minutes, rotating the pan halfway through for even baking, until the biscones are golden brown and fully baked. Let the biscones cool on the pan on a rack.

While the biscones are cooling, make the glaze. Whisk the confectioners' sugar, sorghum, milk, and vanilla together in a small bowl until smooth.

Drizzle the cooled biscones with the glaze. They are best eaten the day they are made.

VARIATIONS

Cranberry Biscones with Orange Zest Glaze
Use ½ cup cranberries instead of the walnuts. Use fresh berries if they are in season; if you use frozen berries, add them unthawed. For the glaze, whisk ¾ cup confectioners' sugar with the grated zest and juice of 1 orange.

Oatmeal Raisin Biscones with Vanilla Glaze
Use whole milk instead of buttermilk. Substitute ½ cup raisins and ½ cup old-fashioned oats for the walnuts. For the glaze, whisk together ¾ cup confectioners' sugar and 1 teaspoon vanilla.

EGGNOG FRENCH TOAST

Serves 6

The holidays would not be complete without my Eggnog French Toast. The eggnog gives the toast a richer, more custardy texture, and the nutmeg and cinnamon add a little kick of spice. I sprinkle it with confectioners' sugar and serve it with one of my handmade syrups (I like the Blackberry Syrup) and a side of bacon and fresh fruit.

6 large eggs
1½ cups eggnog
1 tablespoon pure vanilla extract
2 teaspoons grated orange zest
¼ teaspoon ground cinnamon

¼ teaspoon freshly grated nutmeg
Pinch of fine sea salt
6 thick slices bread, such as crusty baguette or challah
4 tablespoons unsalted butter

¼ cup olive oil

Confectioners' sugar for dusting
Warm Blackberry Syrup (page 290) or maple syrup

In a medium mixing bowl, whisk together the eggs, eggnog, vanilla, orange zest, cinnamon, nutmeg, and salt.

Place the bread slices in a baking dish large enough to hold them in a single layer. Pour the egg mixture over the bread and let soak for 10 to 15 minutes. Flip the bread over to make sure it is completely soaked in the liquid.

Preheat the oven to 250°F.

In a large heavy-bottomed skillet, heat half of the butter and half of the olive oil over medium heat until the butter begins to sizzle. Gently place 3 slices of the soaked bread in the skillet and cook for 2 to 3 minutes per side, until golden brown.

Transfer the slices to a baking sheet and keep warm in the oven while you cook the remaining slices in the remaining butter and oil.

Sprinkle the French toast with confectioners' sugar and serve with warm syrup.

PANCAKES WITH BUTTERED MAPLE PECAN SYRUP

Each batch makes 14 to 16 small pancakes

Sunday is my favorite day of the week. You'd think Griff and I wouldn't cook then, but I love to make a relaxing brunch at home on our day off. I always keep a big jar of my homemade pancake mix in the pantry, so I can fix pancakes at any time—I only need to add the wet ingredients when it's time to cook. I like to make small pancakes so I can stack them up tall on my plate and top them with warm Buttered Maple Pecan Syrup.

FOR THE PANCAKE MIX
4 cups unbleached all-purpose flour
3 tablespoons baking powder, preferably aluminum-free
3 tablespoons granulated sugar
2 teaspoons baking soda
1 teaspoon fine sea salt

FOR EACH 1 CUP PANCAKE MIX
1 large egg
1 cup buttermilk
1 tablespoon unsalted butter, melted

Nonstick spray or unsalted butter for cooking
Buttered Maple Pecan Syrup (recipe follows)

To make the pancake mix: In a large mixing bowl, whisk together the flour, baking powder, sugar, baking soda, and salt. The mix can be stored in an airtight jar for up to 3 months.

Preheat the oven to 200°F. Heat an electric griddle to 375°F or heat a cast-iron griddle over medium-high heat. You can check to make sure the griddle is hot enough by flicking a few drops of water onto it: if the water bounces and sizzles, you are ready to go.

Meanwhile, in a small bowl, whisk together the egg, buttermilk, and melted butter.

Scoop 1 cup of the pancake mix into a medium mixing bowl and whisk in the liquid ingredients. It is important not to overmix your batter: you want to mix just until the ingredients are incorporated. The idea is to leave some small lumps in the batter, which will make for light and fluffy pancakes.

Spray the griddle with nonstick spray or melt 1 tablespoon of butter on it. Spoon 1 or 2 tablespoons of batter onto the hot griddle for each pancake and cook until the edges begin to set and small bubbles appear on top. Peek underneath one to make sure the bottom is golden. Flip and cook for about another minute. Transfer to a heatproof platter and keep warm in the oven while you cook the rest of the pancakes.

Serve the pancakes warm with the maple pecan syrup.

Buttered Maple Pecan Syrup | *Makes about 2 cups*

1 cup pecans
4 tablespoons unsalted butter
2 cups pure maple syrup
1 teaspoon ground ginger
¼ teaspoon freshly grated nutmeg

Position a rack in the middle of the oven and preheat the oven to 350°F.

Spread the nuts out in a single layer in a baking sheet and bake for 5 to 7 minutes, until the edges of the nuts begin to darken. Transfer to a plate and let cool, then finely chop.

In a medium saucepan, melt the butter over medium heat. Add the syrup, ginger, and nutmeg and stir to combine. Add the toasted pecans and stir for 2 to 3 minutes. Serve warm.

The syrup can be stored in an airtight container in the refrigerator for up to 2 weeks. Reheat over low heat before serving.

BREAKFAST BREAD PUDDING

• *Serves 8* •

This savory bread pudding reminds Griff of the Minnesota hot dishes that he grew up eating. It's a simple do-ahead recipe I make for brunch, but with the bacon, mushrooms, and Fontina, it's hearty enough for lunch or dinner too. To make a complete meal, serve the bread pudding with a small salad and some fresh fruit.

2 tablespoons unsalted butter

½ pound portabello mushrooms, sliced

1 medium sweet onion, diced

3 garlic cloves, finely chopped

Fine sea salt and freshly ground black pepper

¾ pound applewood-smoked bacon, cut into ¼-inch pieces

1 pound Fontina cheese, shredded

½ cup grated Parmigiano-Reggiano cheese

¼ teaspoon red pepper flakes

1 teaspoon rubbed sage (see Tip)

6 large eggs

2½ cups half-and-half

1 pound ciabatta (day-old is best), cut into 1-inch cubes

Position a rack in the middle of the oven and preheat the oven to 350°F. Use 1 tablespoon of the butter to coat a 9-by-13-inch baking dish.

In a large heavy skillet, melt the remaining 1 tablespoon butter over medium heat. Add the mushrooms and onion and sauté until the liquid the mushrooms release has reduced and the vegetables are tender, about 8 minutes. Add the garlic and sauté for 1 minute; stir to combine. Transfer to a medium bowl and season with salt and pepper to taste. Set aside.

In the same skillet, cook the bacon over medium heat until crisp and browned, about 10 minutes. Using a slotted spoon, transfer the bacon to the bowl of onions and mushrooms; reserve 2 tablespoons of the bacon fat. Add the Fontina, Parmigiano-Reggiano, red pepper flakes, and rubbed sage and stir to combine.

In a large mixing bowl, whisk the eggs, then add the half-and-half and the reserved bacon fat and whisk until combined.

Spread half of the bread in the prepared baking dish. Spread half of the onion-mushroom mixture evenly over the bread. Top with the remaining bread and another layer of the remaining onion-mushroom mixture. Pour the egg mixture evenly over the top. Using the back of a spoon, press the bread into the liquid, making sure all the liquid is absorbed. Let sit for 15 minutes before baking. (The bread pudding can be covered with plastic wrap, refrigerated, and baked the next day.)

Bake the bread pudding for 40 to 50 minutes, until evenly browned on top. Let rest for 5 minutes before serving.

Tip: Rubbed sage, crushed and crumbled dried sage leaves, adds a warm earthy-woody flavor to any dish. It can be found in the spice section of any grocery store.

GOOD-MORNING GRANOLA

Makes 7 cups

Everyone should have a homemade granola in their repertoire. Mine is made with oats, walnuts, coconut, and usually cocoa nibs. I eat it for breakfast with milk, grab a fistful to eat as an energizing snack during the day, or layer it into a yogurt parfait to enjoy anytime. When you make granola yourself, you know exactly what goes into the recipe; you can make it healthful and you can customize it. If you're allergic to nuts, leave them out; if you want it a little sweeter, swap in chocolate chips for the cocoa nibs.

2½ cups old-fashioned rolled oats (not quick-cooking)
½ cup barley flakes
1 tablespoon wheat bran (optional)
⅔ cup raw walnuts, coarsely chopped

⅓ cup raw pine nuts
1 cup unsweetened flaked coconut
2 tablespoons cocoa nibs
1 teaspoon fine sea salt
½ teaspoon ground allspice
⅓ cup canola oil
¼ cup maple syrup

¼ cup molasses
¼ cup packed dark brown sugar
1 tablespoon pure vanilla extract
½ cup dried cherries
½ cup golden raisins

Position a rack in the middle of the oven and preheat the oven to 300°F. Line a baking sheet with parchment.

In a large mixing bowl, combine the rolled oats, barley flakes, wheat bran, if using, walnuts, pine nuts, coconut, cocoa nibs, sea salt, and allspice and toss well.

In a small saucepan, combine the canola oil, maple syrup, molasses, vanilla, and brown sugar. Cook over low heat, stirring, until the sugar is dissolved and the ingredients are well combined. Remove from the heat and pour over the dry ingredients, stirring to coat the dry ingredients.

Transfer to the prepared pan and use a spatula to spread the granola evenly in the pan. Bake for 30 minutes. Give the granola a toss, turn the pan around so the granola browns evenly, and bake for an additional 10 to 15 minutes, until golden brown. Let cool completely. Add the dried cherries and raisins to the granola and toss well.

The granola can be stored in an airtight container for up to 4 weeks.

MARSHMALLOW CHANDELIER

Our marshmallow chandelier has become famous: folks always get a kick out of seeing the strands and strands of the dreamy confections dangling from our dining room ceiling. It started as a holiday decoration in the middle of what we call "marshmallow season" one year, and then we fell in love with it and couldn't bear to take it down.

This project, which uses cupcake liners to make pom-pom flowers, paper straws, and lots of marshmallows, of course, makes a mobile chandelier that is perfect for a party. *Makes 1 chandelier*

MATERIALS

75 paper cupcake liners in different sizes: mini, regular, and jumbo
Craft paper and cardstock in your choice of colors
Baker's twine
Metal hoop 18 to 22 inches in diameter (a disassembled lampshade armature is perfect)
100 paper straws
Key ring
One 10½-ounce bag mini marshmallows
One 16-ounce bag large marshmallows

TOOLS

Stapler
1- to 2-inch star punch
Scissors
Large-eyed upholstery needle
Glue gun

Step 1: Stack 3 or 4 cupcake liners of varying sizes and staple together in the center. Repeat until you have 10 to 15 flowers.

Step 2: Punch 200 stars from the craft paper and cardstock.

Step 3: Tie eight 22-inch-long pieces of twine to the metal hoop, spacing them evenly.

Step 4: Cut the straws into 1½-inch sections. Using the upholstery needle, thread the straws and stars onto the twine, alternating straws and stars.

Step 5: Pull up the loose ends of the twine and knot them onto the key ring; your chandelier will hang from the key ring, so be sure the twine is securely fastened.

Step 6: Hang your chandelier in a place you can reach easily so you can continue building it. Attach four 28-inch-long pieces of twine to the hoop, one between every pair of top strands. Using the needle and twine, attach some of the marshmallows and the remaining stars and straws to these pieces of twine, alternating them, then attach the loose ends, creating overlapping swags.

Step 7: String the remaining marshmallows and the small liners to create "bells." Tie them between the swags.

Step 8: Using hot glue, attach the cupcake liner flowers at the tied twine-and-hoop intersections.

Step 9: Find the ideal spot to hang your centerpiece, and bring it out when you want a festive decoration for a birthday or holiday party—or leave it hanging all year long!

EVERYDAY CAKES

EASY RECIPES FOR DRESSED-DOWN TREATS

I have baked all my life. In my twenties, I was the girl who would bake every Sunday afternoon, making treats to take to the office for my coworkers on Monday morning. I'd lovingly tie a box with twine and seal it with my handmade labels to stock our break-room pantry. I was working in an architect's office, surrounded by creative folks who put in long hours, and they always appreciated my efforts. As for me, I found so much pleasure in making things by hand, and it was a great way to wind down on a Sunday. I also loved shopping in thrift stores—I always felt like I was on a treasure hunt. And I loved the small local hangouts in my neighborhood. But I never realized how my different passions would mingle. I used to daydream in vivid detail about owning my own vintage-style restaurant someday—a place that would make everyone feel as comfortable as I did visiting my favorite spots in Los Angeles.

Fast-forward twenty years: I own my own bakery and I can happily bring all those parts of my world under one roof. At our bakery, every day feels like a special occasion, and that makes me very happy—and it makes our customers happy too. It is so much fun to see magical moments happen right before my eyes. In my world, cakes aren't just for celebrating birthdays or big life events. And I think this is all part of what makes our bakery such a unique place. On any given day, you will find our pastry cases filled with all kinds of simple cakes, from Bundt cakes to pound cakes to coffee cakes, because

who needs a holiday to enjoy a piece of cake? Some days you just want a little slice of sweetness to go with your morning coffee or to carry back to your desk.

This chapter includes some of our favorite cakes that you can whip up in just a little bit of time, any day of the week. These are the ones our customers request day after day, such as the Very Berry Bundt Cake (page 55), Lemon Poppy Seed Cake (page 76), and Cocoa-Cola Cake (page 62). You can also make them ahead to enjoy for a few days, or give. One of my favorite hostess gifts is the Clementine Pound Cake (page 71). I put it in a basket lined with a vintage linen, to be enjoyed by the hostess the day *after* the party.

SPICE CAKE WITH BUTTERSCOTCH ICING

This is a delicious old-timey recipe inspired by our mentor, Jane Thompson. Jane used to own Mondo Bakery in Atlanta and she taught us how to run a bakery. Her spice cake was one of the first recipes she shared with us. It's an applesauce cake, made with lots of spices, cocoa powder, and apricots and walnuts, and it is absolutely delicious.

Serves 12 to 16

4 cups unbleached all-purpose flour

¼ cup unsweetened cocoa powder

1 tablespoon baking soda

1½ teaspoons fine sea salt

1 teaspoon ground cinnamon

1 teaspoon ground cloves

1 teaspoon freshly grated nutmeg

1 teaspoon ground allspice

½ pound (2 sticks) unsalted butter, at room temperature

3 cups granulated sugar

4 large eggs, at room temperature

3 cups applesauce

1½ cups walnuts

1½ cups dried apricots, coarsely chopped

1 recipe Butterscotch Icing (recipe follows)

Position a rack in the middle of the oven and preheat the oven to 350°F. Spray a 10-inch Bundt pan with nonstick baking spray, making sure to get into all the crevices.

Sift together the flour, cocoa powder, baking soda, salt, cinnamon, cloves, nutmeg, and allspice. Set aside.

In the bowl of a stand mixer fitted with the paddle attachment (or in a large mixing bowl, using a handheld mixer), cream the butter and sugar together on medium-high speed for 4 to 5 minutes, until light and fluffy. Add the eggs one at a time, mixing well after each addition and scraping down the sides of the bowl with a rubber spatula as necessary.

With the mixer on low speed, add the sifted dry ingredients in thirds, alternating with the applesauce and beginning and ending with flour.

Remove the bowl from the mixer and gently fold in the walnuts and apricots. Scrape the batter into the prepared pan and spread it evenly with a spatula.

Bake for 50 to 60 minutes, until a cake tester inserted in the center of the cake comes out clean. Let the cake cool in the pan on a wire rack for 20 minutes, then invert it onto the rack and cool completely.

Once the cake has cooled, transfer it to a serving plate. Frost the top of the cake with the icing, letting it drip down the sides of the cake too so that everyone gets plenty of frosting in every bite.

The cake can be stored in an airtight container at room temperature for up to 5 days. It will get better every day as the spices make one happy marriage.

BUTTERSCOTCH ICING | *Makes about 2½ cups*

8 tablespoons (1 stick) unsalted butter
⅔ cup packed dark brown sugar
½ cup heavy cream
3 cups confectioners' sugar
1 teaspoon pure vanilla extract

In a medium saucepan, melt the butter over medium heat. Add the brown sugar and whisk until the sugar has completely dissolved, about 3 minutes. Gradually add the cream, then continue whisking until smooth, 2 to 3 minutes. Transfer to the bowl of a stand mixer (or to a large bowl if using a handheld mixer) and let cool for 10 to 15 minutes, stirring occasionally.

Using the paddle attachment (or handheld mixer), mixing on medium speed, gradually add the confectioners' sugar and vanilla, then continue beating until the icing is slightly lighter in color and light and creamy in texture. Use immediately.

VERY BERRY BUNDT CAKE WITH BUTTERMILK GLAZE

Serves 12 to 16

Bundt cakes are close to our hearts because the original Bundt pan was made by a cookware company called Nordic Ware, based in Griff's home state of Minnesota. Griff grew up eating all types of Bundt cakes, as did I. A Bundt pan handles heavy cake batters with ease, and its design allows the cakes to come out easily. Studded with fresh berries and topped with a buttermilk glaze, this is the cake to serve with cups of steaming-hot coffee next time you have friends over for a catch-up.

2½ cups unbleached all-purpose flour

2 teaspoons baking powder, preferably aluminum-free

½ teaspoon baking soda

½ teaspoon fine sea salt

½ teaspoon ground cardamom

¼ cup buttermilk, at room temperature

2 teaspoons pure vanilla extract

½ pound (2 sticks) unsalted butter, at room temperature

2 cups granulated sugar

3 large eggs, at room temperature

1 cup sour cream, at room temperature

¾ cup blueberries

¾ cup raspberries

FOR THE BUTTERMILK GLAZE

1 cup granulated sugar

¼ cup heavy cream

3 tablespoons unsalted butter

1 tablespoon honey

½ cup buttermilk

1 teaspoon pure vanilla extract

Position a rack in the middle of the oven and preheat the oven to 350°F. Spray a 10-inch Bundt pan with nonstick baking spray, making sure to get into the tight crevices.

Sift together the flour, baking powder, baking soda, salt, and cardamom. Set aside.

In a measuring cup or a small bowl, mix together the buttermilk and vanilla.

In the bowl of a stand mixer fitted with the paddle attachment (or in a large mixing bowl, using a handheld mixer), cream the butter and sugar together on medium-high speed for 4 to 5 minutes, until light and fluffy. Add the eggs one at a time, mixing well after each addition and scraping down the sides of the bowl with a rubber spatula as necessary. Add the sour cream and mix just until blended, about 1 minute.

continued

With the mixer on low speed, add the flour mixture in thirds, alternating with the buttermilk mixture and beginning and ending with flour.

Remove the bowl from the mixer and gently fold in the berries. Scrape the batter into the prepared pan and spread it evenly with a spatula.

Bake for 50 to 60 minutes, until a cake tester inserted in the center of the cake comes out clean. Let the cake cool in the pan on a wire rack for 20 minutes, then invert it onto the rack and cool completely.

Meanwhile, make the glaze: In a small saucepan, combine the sugar, cream, butter, and honey and bring to a gentle boil over medium heat, stirring to dissolve the sugar. Reduce the heat to low and simmer for about 3 minutes, stirring occasionally. Remove from the heat and whisk in the buttermilk and vanilla. Let the glaze cool until tepid.

Transfer the cake to a serving plate. Use a spoon to drizzle the glaze over the top of the cake.

The cake can be stored in an airtight container at room temperature for up to 2 days.

MEXICAN SPICE CAKE WITH CHOCOLATE GLAZE

Serves 12 to 16

Griff and I make up new recipes all the time: we might take inspiration from a savory meal at a restaurant, from a new spice, or from our travels. While there is no beer in this cake, we came up with the recipe after trying the sought-after Mexican Cake Beer made by Westbrook Brewing Company, in Charleston, South Carolina. It's an imperial stout beer aged with cocoa nibs, vanilla beans, cinnamon sticks, and chile peppers, which are all flavors in this cake.

¼ cup hot water
⅓ cup Dutch-processed cocoa powder
3 large eggs
1½ teaspoons pure vanilla extract
¾ cup plus 2 tablespoons unbleached all-purpose flour
1 teaspoon baking powder, preferably aluminum-free

½ teaspoon ground cinnamon
¼ teaspoon cayenne pepper
Pinch of fine sea salt
12 tablespoons (1½ sticks) unsalted butter, at room temperature
1 cup granulated sugar
10 ounces (1⅔ cups) bittersweet chocolate chunks
2 tablespoons cocoa nibs

FOR THE CHOCOLATE GLAZE
¼ cup heavy cream
4 tablespoons unsalted butter, cut into cubes
2 tablespoons granulated sugar
Pinch of fine sea salt
4 ounces bittersweet chocolate, finely chopped
½ teaspoon pure vanilla extract

Position a rack in the middle of the oven and preheat the oven to 350°F. Spray a 9-by-9-by-2-inch cake pan with nonstick spray. Lightly dust the pan with flour, tapping the pan on the counter to shake out the excess.

In a small mixing bowl, stir together the hot water and cocoa powder to make a stiff paste. Add the eggs and vanilla and stir until combined; the mixture will look a bit lumpy. Set aside.

In another small bowl, whisk together the flour, baking powder, cinnamon, cayenne, and salt. Set aside.

In the bowl of a stand mixer fitted with the paddle attachment (or in a large mixing bowl, using a handheld mixer), cream the butter and sugar on medium-high speed for 3 to 5 minutes, until light and fluffy. Turn the mixer speed down to low and add the flour mixture in thirds, beating well after each addition and scraping down the sides of the bowl with a rubber spatula as necessary. Add the cocoa mixture and mix on medium-high for another minute to lighten the batter.

Remove the bowl from the mixer and, using a rubber spatula, fold in the chocolate chunks and cocoa nibs. Pour the batter into the prepared pan.

Bake for 40 to 45 minutes, until a cake tester inserted in the center of the cake comes out clean. Let the cake cool in the pan on a wire rack for 20 minutes, then invert onto the rack, turn right side up, and let cool completely.

To make the chocolate glaze: In a large heatproof bowl, combine the cream, butter, sugar, and salt, set over a saucepan of barely simmering water (do not let the bottom of the bowl touch the water), and stir until the butter is melted. Add the chocolate and stir until the chocolate has melted and the mixture is completely smooth. Remove from the heat. Stir in the vanilla.

Transfer the cake to a serving plate. Pour the chocolate glaze over the cake, letting it run down the sides. Let it set before slicing and serving.

The cake can be stored in an airtight container at room temperature for up to 3 days.

ANGEL FOOD CAKE WITH WHIPPED CREAM AND BERRIES

Serves 12 to 16

I will admit, angel food cake is second only to chocolate cake in my affections. I adore the delicate texture of the cake crumb, and I like to top slices with fresh summer berries and slather them with sweetened whipped cream—heaven on a plate. The egg whites are the key to making an angel food cake. To separate your eggs cleanly, do it when they are cold. Then let the whites come up to room temperature before you start. The yolks can go back into the fridge for another use (but be sure to use them within two days).

1⅓ cups cake flour (not self-rising)
2 cups superfine sugar
½ teaspoon fine sea salt

1½ cups egg whites (about 12), at room temperature
1 teaspoon cream of tartar

2 teaspoons pure vanilla extract

1 recipe Fresh Whipped Cream (recipe follows)
Fresh berries for garnish

Position a rack in the lower third of the oven and preheat the oven to 350°F.

Using a sifter or a fine-mesh sieve, sift the flour, ½ cup of the sugar, and the salt together three times. Set aside.

In the impeccably clean bowl of a stand mixer fitted with the whisk attachment (or in a large mixing bowl, using a handheld mixer), beat the egg whites and cream of tartar on medium speed until frothy, about 2 minutes. Add the remaining 1½ cups sugar 1 tablespoon at a time, beating on high speed, then beat until the egg whites are stiff and shiny. Add the vanilla and whip just until combined. Remove the bowl from the mixer.

Gently but thoroughly fold the flour mixture about one-quarter at a time into the egg whites. Spoon the batter into an ungreased 10-inch tube pan. (Don't be tempted to smack the pan against the kitchen counter to level the batter; you want to retain all of that air you just incorporated into your egg whites.)

Bake the cake for 35 to 40 minutes, until it is golden brown and a skewer inserted in the center comes out clean. Invert the cake pan onto its feet onto the counter. If the pan does not have feet, invert it over a long-necked bottle, such as a wine bottle. (Cooling the cake upside down prevents it from deflating.) Let cool completely, about 1 hour.

continued

Run a knife around the edges of the pan and the center tube to release the cake with ease and put it top side up on a serving plate. Serve with the whipped cream, garnished with berries.

The cake can be stored in an airtight container at room temperature for up to 3 days.

Fresh Whipped Cream | *Makes about 3 cups*

2 cups heavy cream
¼ cup confectioners' sugar

In the bowl of a stand mixer fitted with the whisk attachment (or in a large mixing bowl, using a handheld mixer), whip the cream on medium speed until it starts to thicken. Add the confectioners' sugar and beat until the cream holds nice soft peaks.

COCOA-COLA CAKE WITH CHOCOLATE ICING

*Serves
12 to 16*

This cake is full of chocolate goodness, inside and out, and both the cake and the frosting get a good dose of Coca-Cola. Be sure to use the real thing—diet soda will not work here! Mini marshmallows melt over the hot cake and are topped with chocolate icing and pecans.

Serve the kids the chocolaty cake with a glass of ice-cold milk; they'll race home from school to get this afternoon snack.

2 cups unbleached all-
   purpose flour
¼ cup Dutch-processed
   cocoa powder
1 teaspoon baking soda
1 cup Coca-Cola, at room
   temperature
½ cup buttermilk
2 tablespoons pure vanilla
   extract

1¾ cups granulated sugar
½ pound (2 sticks)
   unsalted butter, at room
   temperature
2 large eggs, at room
   temperature

1½ cups mini
   marshmallows

FOR THE CHOCOLATE ICING

8 tablespoons (1 stick)
   unsalted butter, melted
5 tablespoons unsweetened
   cocoa powder
⅓ cup Coca-Cola
1 teaspoon pure vanilla
   extract
One 16-ounce box
   confectioners' sugar
1 cup chopped pecans

Position a rack in the middle of the oven and preheat the oven to 350°F. Lightly spray a 9-by-13-by-2-inch baking pan with nonstick spray. Line with parchment, leaving an overhang on two opposite sides of the pan.

Sift the flour, cocoa, and baking soda together. Set aside.

In a small bowl, mix together the cola, buttermilk, and vanilla. Set aside.

In the bowl of a stand mixer fitted with the paddle attachment (or in a large mixing bowl, using a handheld mixer), cream the sugar and butter on medium-high speed for 4 to 5 minutes, until light and fluffy. Add the eggs one at a time, mixing well after each addition and scraping down the sides of the bowl with a rubber spatula as necessary.

Turn the mixer speed down to low and add the flour mixture in thirds, alternating with the Coca-Cola mixture and beginning and ending with flour. Remove the bowl from the mixer and, using the rubber spatula, incorporate any ingredients hiding at the bottom of the bowl, making sure the

batter is completely mixed. Scrape the batter into the prepared pan and spread it evenly with a spatula.

Bake for 30 to 35 minutes, until a cake tester inserted in the center of the cake comes out clean. Scatter the marshmallows over the top of the hot cake and return to the oven for about 2 minutes, until they are melted.

In the meantime, make the chocolate icing: In a medium bowl, combine the melted butter, cocoa, Coca-Cola, and vanilla and mix with a spoon until smooth and creamy. Gradually add the confectioners' sugar, mixing until the icing is completely smooth. Fold in the pecans.

When the cake is done, remove from the oven and let cool on a wire rack for 10 minutes.

Spread the frosting over the warm cake. It will firm up as the cake cools.

The cake can be stored in an airtight container at room temperature for up to 3 days.

BANANA CHIFFON CAKE WITH BANANA–CREAM CHEESE FROSTING

Bananas are one of those fruits that everyone loves and that go well with anything. This light and fluffy cake improves upon an already good thing. Put mashed bananas in the batter and top the cake with a banana–cream cheese frosting, and banana lovers will rejoice.

Serves 12 to 16

2 cups cake flour (not self-rising)

1⅓ cups granulated sugar

1 teaspoon baking powder, preferably aluminum-free

1 teaspoon baking soda

1 teaspoon fine sea salt

2 large eggs, separated, at room temperature

1 large egg white

¼ teaspoon cream of tartar

¾ cup buttermilk

⅓ cup canola oil

1 teaspoon pure vanilla extract

1 cup mashed extra-ripe bananas (about 2½ large bananas)

1 recipe Banana–Cream Cheese Frosting (recipe follows)

Position a rack in the lower third of the oven and preheat the oven to 350°F. Butter a 9-by-13-by-2-inch baking pan, then line the bottom with parchment and butter it as well. Lightly dust the pan with flour, tapping the pan on the counter to shake out the excess.

Sift together the cake flour, 1 cup of the sugar, the baking powder, baking soda, and salt into a large mixing bowl. Set aside.

In the bowl of a stand mixer fitted with the whisk attachment (or in a large mixing bowl, using a handheld mixer), beat the egg whites and cream of tartar until frothy. Gradually add the remaining ⅓ cup sugar and continue to whip until stiff peaks form. Set aside.

Make a well in the center of the dry ingredients. Add half of the buttermilk, the oil, vanilla, and mashed bananas and stir for 1 to 2 minutes, until the ingredients are thoroughly combined. Add the egg yolks and the rest of the buttermilk, stirring until just combined. Gently fold in the egg whites.

Scrape the batter into the prepared pan and gently smooth the top with a spatula. Tap the pan firmly on the counter to remove any air bubbles from the batter.

continued

Bake for 40 to 50 minutes, until a cake tester inserted in the center of the cake comes out clean. Let the cake cool for 15 minutes, then remove from the pan, peel off the parchment, and cool completely on a wire rack.

Put the cake on a plate and frost the top and sides with the cream cheese frosting, making big swirls with an offset spatula or a butter knife.

The cake can be refrigerated for up to 5 days. Bring to room temperature before serving.

BANANA–CREAM CHEESE FROSTING | *Makes about 3 cups*

1 extra-ripe banana
One 8-ounce package cream cheese, cut into chunks, at room temperature
4 tablespoons unsalted butter, at room temperature
1 teaspoon pure vanilla extract
3 to 4 cups confectioners' sugar

In a small saucepan, mash the banana and cook until it becomes liquid and begins to thicken a bit, 3 to 5 minutes. Set aside to cool.

In the bowl of a stand mixer fitted with the paddle attachment (or in a medium mixing bowl, using a handheld mixer), beat the cream cheese, butter, and vanilla on medium speed until smooth and creamy, 3 to 5 minutes. Add the cooled banana and mix until completely incorporated, scraping down the sides of the bowl with a rubber spatula as necessary. With the mixer on low speed, gradually add 3 cups of the confectioners' sugar, then gradually add up to 1 cup more sugar if the frosting seems thin, and continue beating until light and fluffy, 3 to 5 minutes.

The frosting can be refrigerated in an airtight container for up to 5 days. When ready to use it, let the frosting come to room temperature and whip by hand until it is light and fluffy again.

GINNY'S CHOCOLATE CHIP CAKE WITH CLASSIC CHOCOLATE BUTTERCREAM

Griff's mom always baked a cake at the beginning of each week for her family to snack on. As one of the favorites at the Day household, this recipe was at the front of her recipe box. It's a simple, quick cake that's frosted generously with chocolate buttercream.

Serves 9 to 12

1 cup whole milk

1 teaspoon pure vanilla extract

1¾ cups cake flour (not self-rising)

1¼ cups unbleached all-purpose flour

1 tablespoon baking powder, preferably aluminum-free

¾ teaspoon fine sea salt

½ pound (2 sticks) unsalted butter, at room temperature

1½ cups granulated sugar

½ cup packed light brown sugar

4 large eggs, at room temperature

1 cup semisweet chocolate chips

1 recipe Classic Chocolate Buttercream (recipe follows)

Position a rack in the middle of the oven and preheat the oven to 350°F. Butter a 9-by-13-by-2-inch baking pan, then line with parchment, leaving an overhang on the two long sides of the pan. Butter the parchment as well and dust with flour, tapping out the excess.

In a measuring cup or a small bowl, mix together the milk and vanilla. Set aside.

Sift together both flours, the baking powder, and salt. Set aside.

In the bowl of a stand mixer fitted with the paddle attachment (or in a large mixing bowl, using a handheld mixer), cream the butter and both sugars together on medium-high speed for 3 to 5 minutes, until light and fluffy. Turn the mixer speed down to low and add the eggs one at a time, beating well after each addition and scraping down the sides of the bowl with a rubber spatula as necessary.

continued

With the mixer on low speed, add the flour mixture in thirds, alternating with the milk and beginning and ending with flour. Remove the bowl from the mixer and gently fold in the chocolate chips. Using the rubber spatula, incorporate any ingredients hiding at the bottom of the bowl, making sure the batter is completely mixed.

Scrape the batter into the prepared pan and gently smooth the top with a spatula. Tap the pan firmly on the counter to remove any air bubbles from the batter.

Bake for 35 to 40 minutes, until a cake tester inserted in the center of the cake comes out clean. Let the cake cool for 15 minutes, then remove it from the pan, using the parchment, invert it onto a wire rack, and peel off the parchment. Let cool completely.

Invert the cake onto a platter and frost the top and sides with the buttercream frosting.

The cake can be stored in an airtight container at room temperature for up to 3 days.

CLASSIC CHOCOLATE BUTTERCREAM | *Makes about 3 cups*

4 ounces semisweet chocolate, finely chopped, or ⅔ cup semisweet chocolate chips
12 tablespoons (1½ sticks) unsalted butter, at room temperature
1 tablespoon whole milk
½ teaspoon pure vanilla extract
1½ cups confectioners' sugar, sifted

Put the chocolate in a heatproof bowl, set it over a saucepan of simmering water (do not let the bottom of the bowl touch the water), and stir occasionally until the chocolate is completely melted. Set the chocolate aside to cool until tepid.

In the bowl of a stand mixer fitted with the paddle attachment (or in a medium mixing bowl, using a handheld mixer), beat the butter on medium speed for 2 to 3 minutes, until smooth and creamy. Add the milk, mixing until completely blended. Add the cooled chocolate and mix until completely incorporated, scraping down the sides of the bowl with a rubber spatula as necessary. Beat in the vanilla. With the mixer on low speed, gradually add the confectioners' sugar and then continue beating until the buttercream is creamy and silky.

The frosting can be stored in an airtight container at room temperature for up to 2 days.

CLEMENTINE POUND CAKE WITH CHOCOLATE HONEY GLAZE

I love to bake with all types of citrus fruits in the winter, when apple season is over and berry season has yet to begin, and one of my favorites to bake with is the clementine. This cake is scented with clementine zest and the glaze is made with two different chocolates. The combination of orange and chocolate is a classic one, and there's a reason for that: the clementine's sweet tartness and the rich flavor of chocolate make a lovely pairing. Serve this as a satisfying after-dinner treat.

Serves 8 to 10

1½ cups cake flour (not self-rising)
½ teaspoon baking powder, preferably aluminum-free
¼ teaspoon baking soda
½ teaspoon fine sea salt
1¼ cups granulated sugar
1 tablespoon grated clementine zest
12 tablespoons (1½ sticks) unsalted butter, at room temperature

5 ounces cream cheese, at room temperature
3 large eggs, at room temperature
1 teaspoon pure vanilla extract

FOR THE CHOCOLATE HONEY GLAZE
½ cup heavy cream
2 tablespoons honey

2 ounces semisweet chocolate, finely chopped, or ⅓ cup semisweet chocolate chips
2 ounces bittersweet chocolate, finely chopped, or ⅓ cup bittersweet chocolate chips
1 teaspoon pure vanilla extract

Position a rack in the middle of the oven and preheat the oven to 350°F. Spray a 9-by-5-inch loaf pan with nonstick spray and line with parchment, leaving an overhang on the two long sides of the pan. (This will make it easy to remove the cake from the pan.)

Sift together the flour, baking powder, baking soda, and salt. Set aside.

In a small bowl, combine the sugar and clementine zest. Set aside. (Mixing the zest with the sugar will help distribute the zest more evenly in the batter.)

In the bowl of a stand mixer fitted with the paddle attachment (or in a large mixing bowl, using a handheld mixer), cream the butter and cream cheese together on medium speed for 2 to 3 minutes, until smooth. Gradually add the sugar mixture and then beat on medium-high speed until very light and fluffy, 4 to 5 minutes. Add the eggs one at a time, mixing well after each

addition and scraping down the sides of the bowl with a rubber spatula as necessary. Add the vanilla and mix until combined.

With the mixer on low speed, add the flour mixture in thirds, mixing just until incorporated. Remove the bowl from the mixer and, using the rubber spatula, incorporate any ingredients hiding at the bottom of the bowl, making sure the batter is completely mixed.

Scrape the batter into the prepared pan and gently smooth the top with a spatula. Tap the pan firmly on the counter to remove any air bubbles from the batter.

Bake for 50 to 60 minutes, until a cake tester inserted in the center of the cake comes out clean. Let the cake cool in the pan on a wire rack for about 20 minutes, then remove it from the pan, using the parchment, peel off the parchment, and cool completely on the rack.

To make the glaze: In a small saucepan, heat the cream to a gentle boil.

Put the honey in a small mixing bowl and pour the hot cream over the honey. Add both chocolates and stir until completely melted and smooth; the glaze will be shiny and glossy. Stir in the vanilla. Let cool until slightly thickened.

Put the cake on a serving platter and pour the glaze over it, allowing it to drip down on the sides. Let stand until the glaze has set.

The cake can be stored in an airtight container at room temperature for up to 3 days.

STRAWBERRY BUTTERMILK CAKE

Serves 8

When strawberries come into season in the spring, we always pick enough to freeze so we can use them year-round. You don't even need to wash the strawberries before freezing—just leave them in their little basket and put it in a ziplock freezer bag. It might seem odd, but if you don't wash them, you don't add any extra moisture, and they will keep longer. When you're ready to use the berries, just defrost in the fridge and clean and hull them as you would if they were fresh.

1½ cups unbleached all-purpose flour
1½ teaspoons baking powder, preferably aluminum-free
½ teaspoon fine sea salt

6 tablespoons unsalted butter, at room temperature
1 cup granulated sugar
1 large egg, at room temperature
½ cup buttermilk

1 teaspoon pure vanilla extract
1 pound strawberries, hulled and halved

Confectioners' sugar for dusting

Position a rack in the middle of the oven and preheat the oven to 350°F. Lightly butter a 9-inch deep-dish pie pan.

Sift together the flour, baking powder, and salt. Set aside.

In the bowl of a stand mixer fitted with the paddle attachment (or in a large mixing bowl, using a handheld mixer), cream the butter and sugar together on medium-high speed for 3 to 5 minutes, until light and fluffy. Add the egg, buttermilk, and vanilla and mix until blended, about 1 minute.

With the mixer on low speed, gradually add the flour mixture, mixing until just combined.

Remove the bowl from the mixer and, using a rubber spatula, incorporate any ingredients hiding at the bottom of the bowl, making sure the batter is completely mixed. Scrape the batter into the prepared pie plate and gently smooth the top with a spatula. Tap the pan firmly on the counter to remove any air bubbles from the batter. Arrange the strawberries in concentric rings on top of the batter, cut side down.

Bake the cake for 10 minutes, then reduce the temperature to 325°F and bake for 50 to 60 minutes, until a cake tester inserted in the center comes out clean. Let the cake cool in the pan on a wire rack.

Before serving, dust the top of the cake with confectioners' sugar.

The cake can be stored in an airtight container in the refrigerator for up to 2 days.

LEMON POPPY SEED CAKE WITH LEMON GLAZE

Lemon and poppy seeds are a classic combination. If you love lemons as much as I do, then pucker up, because this cake has more than a twist. The lemon syrup and glaze keep it supermoist, and the flavors get better every day. If you keep it on the kitchen counter, you will be tempted to cut a slice every time you pass it.

Serves 12 to 16

1¾ cups unbleached all-purpose flour

1 teaspoon baking powder, preferably aluminum-free

1 teaspoon baking soda

¼ teaspoon fine sea salt

½ pound (2 sticks) unsalted butter, at room temperature

1 cup granulated sugar

1 teaspoon pure vanilla extract

3 large eggs, at room temperature

1 cup sour cream, at room temperature

½ cup poppy seeds

FOR THE SOAKING SYRUP

¾ cup fresh lemon juice (from 4 to 5 lemons)

¾ cup granulated sugar

FOR THE LEMON GLAZE

1½ cups confectioners' sugar

1 tablespoon grated lemon zest

3 tablespoons whole milk

Position a rack in the middle of the oven and preheat the oven to 350°F. Butter a 9-inch springform pan. Line the bottom with parchment and butter it as well. Lightly dust the pan with flour, tapping the pan on the counter to shake out the excess.

Sift together the flour, baking powder, baking soda, and salt. Set aside.

In the bowl of a stand mixer fitted with the paddle attachment (or in a large mixing bowl, using a handheld mixer), cream the butter, sugar, and vanilla together on medium-high speed for 4 to 5 minutes, until light and fluffy. Add the eggs one at a time, mixing well after each addition and scraping down the sides of the bowl with a rubber spatula as necessary.

With the mixer on low speed, gradually add about half of the flour mixture, followed by the sour cream. Add the remaining flour and mix just until incorporated.

Remove the bowl from the mixer and fold in the poppy seeds. Scrape the batter into the prepared pan and spread it evenly with a spatula.

Bake for 50 to 60 minutes, until a cake tester inserted in the center of the cake comes out clean. Let the cake cool in the pan on a wire rack for 15 minutes.

Meanwhile, make the soaking syrup: Combine the lemon juice and sugar in a small nonreactive saucepan and cook over low heat, stirring often, until the sugar dissolves. Then continue cooking until the syrup turns a deep golden yellow, 3 to 4 minutes. Remove from the heat.

Poke holes all over the cake with a skewer. Pour the soaking syrup over the cake until it is completely moistened. Let the cake stand for at least 10 minutes so the syrup is absorbed. Release the springform ring and remove it, then use a metal spatula to release the cake from the parchment and the bottom of the springform pan and transfer it to a serving platter.

To make the glaze: In a small bowl, combine the confectioners' sugar, half of the lemon zest, and the milk and whisk until smooth.

Use a spoon to drizzle the glaze over the top of the cake. Sprinkle the remaining lemon zest over the cake. Let stand until the glaze is set.

The cake can be stored in an airtight container at room temperature for up to 5 days.

APPLE BRANDY BROWN BUTTER– GLAZED CAKE

Serves 12 to 16

This rustic cake is made with a thick batter filled with chopped apples and spices. The splash of brandy adds a slightly caramelized flavor that plays off the ginger and fresh nutmeg. The spices, apples, and brown butter glaze make this a comforting fall dessert. I love the way brown butter (see the Tip) adds flavor to glazes, frostings, and other baked goods. Melting the butter and then letting it cook to remove the water and brown the milk solids gives it a toasty, nutty flavor.

3 Gala or Fuji apples, peeled, cored, and cut into ½-inch dice (about 3 cups)
¼ cup brandy
1¾ cups unbleached all-purpose flour
1½ teaspoons baking soda
1 teaspoon ground cinnamon

¼ teaspoon freshly grated nutmeg
¼ teaspoon ground ginger
¼ teaspoon fine sea salt
2 large eggs, at room temperature
1½ cups packed light brown sugar
½ cup granulated sugar
½ pound (2 sticks) unsalted butter, melted and cooled

FOR THE BROWN BUTTER GLAZE
8 tablespoons (1 stick) unsalted butter, cut into tablespoon-sized pieces
1 cup confectioners' sugar
1 teaspoon pure vanilla extract
4 to 6 tablespoons whole milk

Position a rack in the middle of the oven and preheat the oven to 325°F. Butter a 9-by-13-by-2-inch baking pan. Line it with parchment, leaving an overhang on the two long sides of the pan, and butter the parchment.

Put the apples in a medium bowl, add the brandy, and toss until coated. Set aside.

Sift together the flour, baking soda, cinnamon, nutmeg, ginger, and salt. Set aside.

In the bowl of a stand mixer fitted with the paddle attachment (or in a large mixing bowl, using a handheld mixer), beat the eggs and both sugars on medium-high speed for 3 to 5 minutes, until light in color and smooth. Add the melted butter and mix until incorporated. Reduce the speed to low and add the dry ingredients in thirds, mixing just until incorporated. Remove the bowl from the mixer and fold in the apple and brandy mixture with a rubber spatula.

Use the spatula to incorporate any ingredients hiding at the bottom of the bowl, making sure the batter is completely mixed.

Pour the batter into the prepared pan. Tap the pan firmly on the counter to remove any air bubbles from the batter.

Bake for 40 to 45 minutes, until a cake tester inserted in the center of the cake comes out clean. Cool for 20 minutes in the pan, then invert the cake onto a wire rack, peel off the parchment, invert the cake onto another rack, and cool completely.

To make the brown butter glaze: In a small saucepan, melt the butter over medium heat and then continue to cook until the butter has turned a golden brown color and smells fragrant. Set aside to cool slightly.

In a small bowl, whisk together the confectioners' sugar and vanilla. Whisk in the browned butter until smooth. Whisk in ¼ cup milk, then whisk until smooth enough to drizzle, adding up to 2 more tablespoons milk if necessary.

Pour the glaze over the cooled cake.

The cake can be stored in an airtight container at room temperature for up to 2 days.

Tip: When you make brown butter, use a saucepan that is light in color so you can watch the butter browning. Slice the butter into tablespoon-sized pieces and melt over medium heat, stirring with a heatproof spatula as the butter begins to foam up. Keep stirring to make sure that the flavorful brown bits do not stick to the bottom of the pan, and swirl the pan to look for a golden brown color. Watch carefully, because at a certain point the color changes quickly, and the butter can go from golden to burnt in the blink of an eye.

LEMON PUDDING CAKES

Serves 4

It's magical how these cakes do a little trick during baking: an amazing separation happens so you get a layer of cake on the top and a pudding-like consistency on the bottom. I like these while they're still slightly warm and gooey on the inside. I love the lemon-flavor brightness, and the comfort factor is built right in.

1 cup granulated sugar
¼ cup unbleached all-purpose flour
⅛ teaspoon fine sea salt
4 tablespoons unsalted butter, melted
Grated zest of 1 lemon

⅓ cup fresh lemon juice
3 large eggs, separated
1 large egg yolk
1½ cups buttermilk or whole milk
Confectioners' sugar for dusting

Sliced fresh fruit or berries for serving (optional)

SPECIAL EQUIPMENT
Four 4-inch ramekins

Position a rack in the middle of the oven and preheat the oven to 350°F. Butter the ramekins. Set out a deep roasting pan large enough to hold the ramekins.

In a large mixing bowl, whisk together ¾ cup of the granulated sugar, the flour, and salt until thoroughly combined. Add the melted butter, lemon zest, lemon juice, and egg yolks and whisk until smooth. Whisk in the buttermilk until well combined. Set aside.

In the bowl of a stand mixer fitted with the whisk attachment (or in a medium mixing bowl, using a handheld mixer), beat the egg whites until frothy. Gradually add the remaining ¼ cup granulated sugar and continue to whip until stiff peaks form.

Gently fold the beaten egg whites into the lemon mixture. Divide the batter equally among the ramekins. Put the ramekins in the roasting pan and add enough hot water to the roasting pan to come halfway up the sides of the ramekins.

Carefully transfer the pan to the oven; make sure that the water doesn't get into the batter. Bake for 35 to 40 minutes, until the tops are lightly browned. The cakes will be set around the edges, but the centers will still jiggle slightly. Remove the ramekins from the roasting pan and place on a wire rack.

Serve the cakes slightly warm or chilled, with confectioners' sugar dusted on top and fresh fruit, if desired.

The cakes can be stored, tightly covered, in the refrigerator for up to 2 days.

FRESH PEACH CAKE

Serves 9

I'm always looking for new uses for our delicious Georgia peaches. This homey coffee cake is a great way to show them off. The cinnamon sugar melts into the peaches as they bake on top of the cake. Serve warm, topped with a scoop of vanilla ice cream if you like.

1 cup unbleached all-purpose flour

1 teaspoon baking powder, preferably aluminum-free

10 large peaches, peeled, pitted, and cut in half

1 tablespoon fresh lemon juice

8 tablespoons (1 stick) unsalted butter, at room temperature

½ cup plus 3 tablespoons granulated sugar

½ cup packed light brown sugar

2 large eggs, at room temperature

1 teaspoon pure vanilla extract

½ teaspoon ground cinnamon

Position a rack in the middle of the oven and preheat the oven to 350°F. Butter an 8-inch square cake pan, then line the bottom with parchment and butter it as well. Lightly dust the pan with flour, tapping the pan on the counter to shake out the excess.

Sift together the flour and baking powder. Set aside.

In a large bowl, toss the peaches with the lemon juice. Set aside.

In the bowl of a stand mixer fitted with the paddle attachment (or in a large mixing bowl, using a handheld mixer), cream the butter, ½ cup of the granulated sugar, and the brown sugar on medium-high speed until very light and fluffy, 3 to 5 minutes.

With the mixer on low speed, gradually add the dry ingredients, mixing just until incorporated.

Add the eggs one at a time, mixing well after each addition and scraping down the sides of the bowl with a rubber spatula as necessary. Add the vanilla and mix until just incorporated.

Remove the bowl from the mixer and use the rubber spatula to incorporate any ingredients hiding at the bottom of the bowl, making sure the batter is completely mixed. Scrape the batter into the prepared pan and gently smooth the top with the spatula. Tap the pan firmly on the counter to remove any air bubbles from the batter.

Arrange the peaches on top of the batter, cut side down. Stir together the remaining 3 tablespoons granulated sugar and the cinnamon and sprinkle on top of the peaches.

Bake for about 1 hour, until a cake tester inserted in the center of the cake comes out clean. Cool for 15 minutes, then remove from the pan, peel off the parchment, and transfer to a wire rack to cool. Serve warm or at room temperature.

The cake can be stored in an airtight container at room temperature for up to 3 days.

PINEAPPLE UPSIDE-DOWN CAKE

You can make upside-down cakes with all kinds of fruit, but you just can't beat our take on the classic. We make it in a cast-iron skillet and add bourbon to the salted-caramel pineapple topping. Sprinkle in almonds for added flavor and texture.

Serves 8 to 12

FOR THE CARAMEL PINEAPPLE TOPPING

1 pineapple

6 tablespoons unsalted butter

1 cup packed light brown sugar

1 tablespoon bourbon (rum or vanilla works too)

½ teaspoon fine sea salt

¾ cup sliced almonds, toasted

FOR THE CAKE

1⅓ cups cake flour (not self-rising)

2 teaspoons baking powder, preferably aluminum-free

¾ teaspoon ground cinnamon

1 teaspoon ground ginger

1 teaspoon fine sea salt

2 large eggs, at room temperature

2 teaspoons pure vanilla extract

1 cup granulated sugar

8 tablespoons (1 stick) unsalted butter, at room temperature

1 cup sour cream

SPECIAL EQUIPMENT

One 1-inch round cookie cutter

Preheat the oven to 350°F.

To prepare the pineapple: Slice off the top and bottom of the pineapple to create easy-to-manage flat surfaces. Stand the pineapple up and slice the skin away in long strips following the contours of the fruit, making sure to remove all of the brown eyes. Put the peeled pineapple on its side and cut into ½-inch-thick rounds. Using a 1-inch cookie cutter, remove the core from each slice. Set the pineapple aside on paper towels.

To make the caramel topping: Melt the butter in a 10-inch cast-iron skillet over medium heat, or melt it in a 10-inch round cake pan over low heat. Sprinkle the brown sugar, bourbon, and salt over it and cook, stirring occasionally, until the sugar dissolves and the caramel is golden, about 3 minutes. Remove from the heat.

continued

Arrange the sliced pineapple in a circle on top of the caramel mixture, without overlapping the rings, then fill in the center; you can cut the remaining pieces to fill in the gaps if you like. Sprinkle with the toasted almonds.

To make the cake batter: In a medium bowl, whisk together the flour, baking powder, cinnamon, ginger, and salt. Set aside.

In a small bowl, whisk the eggs and vanilla together. Set aside.

In the bowl of a stand mixer fitted with the paddle attachment (or in a large mixing bowl, using a handheld mixer), cream the sugar and butter together on medium-high speed for 3 to 5 minutes, until light and fluffy. Gradually add the eggs and vanilla, beating well and scraping down the sides of the bowl with a rubber spatula as necessary, then beat until doubled in volume, about 2 minutes.

Turn the mixer speed down to low and add the flour mixture in thirds, alternating with the sour cream and beginning and ending with flour.

Remove the bowl from the mixer and use the rubber spatula to incorporate any ingredients hiding at the bottom of the bowl, making sure the batter is completely mixed. Pour the batter over the pineapple and smooth it with a spatula.

Bake for 50 to 60 minutes, until a cake tester inserted in the center of the cake comes out clean. Let the cake cool in the skillet or cake pan for about 30 minutes.

Run a small knife around the edges of the skillet or pan, then place a large serving plate upside down on top and invert the skillet or pan to release the cake onto the plate. Serve warm or at room temperature.

The cake can be stored in an airtight container at room temperature for up to 3 days.

BABY-CAKE PARTY HAT

The inspiration for this hat came from several sources: one of my favorite children's books, *Jennie's Hat,* by Ezra Jack Keats; all of the sweet Southern ladies in our neighborhood who go to church on Sundays in the most beautiful hats you could ever imagine; and our petite cakes at the bakery, which are embellished with buttercream roses, cake toppers, and my favorite vintage bling.

I think everyone should have a special party hat to celebrate their birthday season—and any other festive occasion, for that matter. I have also been known to make one of these party hats for the bride for her bridal shower, or for my friends to wear at a tea party. The hat becomes a treasured heirloom for anyone lucky enough to receive it. *Makes 1 hat*

MATERIALS

2 round cardboard boxes
  approximately 4 inches in
  diameter and 2 inches high (you
  won't use the lids; save them
  for another rainy-day project)
Glitter glue or white glue
Clear glitter
White and red acrylic paint
One 4-pound box plaster of Paris
24 inches ribbon or twine
2 crepe streamer rolls in different
  colors
Thread
Yellow paper remnants, ½ inch to
  1 inch round (pictured: 2 rounds
  of tissue confetti)
Paper straw
Vintage millinery or silk flowers

TOOLS

Paintbrush
Hot glue gun
1-gallon bucket
Painter's stir stick
Icing spatula or butter knife
Awl or hole punch
Ruler
Scissors
Needle

Step 1: Prep the "cake layers" by turning the boxes upside down on a work surface. With a paintbrush and glitter glue, coat the sides of one box, then sprinkle it generously with clear glitter to create a sugar-frosted-cake effect. Repeat with the second box. Allow to dry.

Step 2: Using a hot glue gun, run a bead of glue around the top edges of one box (still upside down) and put a dollop of glue in the center. Stack the second box on top. You now have a two-tiered cake. Allow to dry.

Step 3: Using a painter's stir stick, mix together enough white and red acrylic paint in a 1-gallon bucket to achieve the shade of pink you desire; you need approximately 2 tablespoons of paint total. Add 4 cups plaster of Paris, then slowly stir in warm water until you achieve a frosting-like consistency. Working quickly, use an icing spatula or a butter knife to apply a layer of frosting to the top of the hat, just as you would frost a cake, creating dips and peaks with your spatula. Then carefully apply frosting around the center of the hat to look as though frosting is spilling from between the two layers of cake, slowly turning the hat to work your way all around it. Allow the hat to dry for 2 to 3 hours.

Step 4: Using an awl or a hole punch, pierce 2 holes on each side of the hat—this is where your ties will attach to the hat: Start about ½ inch from the base on one side of your cake and space the second hole ¼ inch above it. Repeat on the opposite side. Cut the ribbon or twine into two 12-inch pieces and knot one end of each ribbon. Working from the inside of the hat, weave the unknotted end of each ribbon through the top hole and then back through the bottom hole. With scissors, trim the ends of each ribbon at a 45-degree angle.

Step 5: Cut 30-inch lengths of each streamer color, then lay one piece on top of the other. Fold about ¼ inch of one long side over and press the fold with your fingers. Using a needle and a 15-inch-long piece of thread, starting at one end, run a basting stitch along the length, then gather it like a ruffle to create the brim of the hat; make sure the ruffle circumference matches the circumference of your cake. Starting at the back of the hat, attach the ruffle using hot glue, slowly making your way around and adding small amounts of hot glue to secure the brim in place. Allow to dry completely.

Step 6: To make the candle, roll 2 yellow paper remnants between your fingers to create a twisted flame. Apply hot glue to one end of the flame and tuck it into one end of a paper straw. Cut the straw down to 3 inches. Put a dab of glue in the center of your cake top and secure the candle.

Step 7: Adorn the top and sides of your cake with millinery or silk flowers, using hot glue to secure them. Make the prettiest party hat you can imagine!

PIE DAY

PIES, TARTS, AND CRISPS

I first learned to bake pies perched on a step stool by my grandma Hannah's side, watching her mix and roll out the crusts on her big farm-style table. To this day, that is still one of my fondest memories of visiting her in Alabama during the summer. When I got older, I moved on to pie-making marathons with my mom, and now Griff and I love to create new pie recipes at the bakery.

The craft of making pies brings the joys of scratch baking all together into one bowl. It's creative, it's seasonal, and it's a great way to pass on the heritage of Southern baking—just like it was passed on to me as a child. Now it's my goal to mentor young pie enthusiasts and to take fear of pie making out of our culture. I love having my friend India spend the day with me making pies at the bakery. She is fourteen years old, and she is as passionate about baking as I am.

India likes to bring in some of her own personal favorite pie recipes handwritten on recipe cards for me to try. Once when I spilled a little buttermilk on one of the cards, she said, "Oh, that just gives it character, don't you think?" (That's my kind of girl!) We spend the day giggling, sharing stories, and testing recipes, some of which appear in this very chapter.

I say "piiiiie" with a very long *i* (and a Southern drawl). For me, it's such a special word it deserves extra emphasis. The recipes you'll find here include a mix of vintage favorites from my family recipe box, like Rustic Plum Pie (page 93) and Apple Custard Pie (page 98), as well as some new specialties from our bakery cases that Griff and I hope become classics too, such as the Double-Chocolate Mint Chess Pie (page 94), Cherry Potpie (page 110), and Razzleberry Crisp (page 115). You can decide which pie you like the most and award it a Best-in-Show Pie Banner (learn how to make one on page 123). Of course I think every pie is a winner!

RUSTIC PLUM PIE

Serves 8

Picking plums from the tree in our backyard is one of my fondest childhood memories. I knew that after she packed a few in my lunch box, my mother would turn the rest into a pie. Plums are the perfect balance of sweet and tart, making them an incredible filling for this free-form pie. There are many different varieties and colors of plum to choose from these days—mix them up and be creative.

2 pounds ripe firm plums, halved, pitted, and sliced into ½-inch-thick wedges

3 tablespoons granulated sugar

1 teaspoon grated lemon zest

1 disk Extra-Flaky Piecrust (page 120)

½ cup grape jelly

1 tablespoon water

1 large egg, lightly beaten with a pinch of fine sea salt for egg wash

Coarse sugar or raw sugar for sprinkling

Position a rack in the middle of the oven and preheat the oven to 425°F. Line a baking sheet with parchment.

Put the plums in a medium bowl, add the sugar and lemon zest, and toss to coat the fruit.

On a lightly floured work surface, with a lightly floured rolling pin, roll the dough into a 12-inch circle. Place it on the prepared baking sheet.

Spoon the plums into the center of the dough, leaving a 2-inch border all around. Gently fold the edges of the dough over the fruit, overlapping the dough as necessary to create a ruffled effect, and press gently to seal the edges. Brush the piecrust with the egg wash and sprinkle with coarse sugar.

Bake for 25 to 35 minutes, until the crust is golden and the juices are bubbling.

Meanwhile, a few minutes before the pie is baked, heat the grape jelly with the water in a small saucepan, stirring with a spoon it is until smooth and the consistency of syrup. Set aside.

Remove the pie from the oven and brush the fruit with the melted jelly so it glistens. Let it cool for at least 5 minutes. Serve slightly warm or at room temperature.

The pie can be stored at room temperature for up to 1 day or refrigerated for up to 2 days.

DOUBLE-CHOCOLATE MINT CHESS PIE

Anything that starts with chocolate and gets a hint of cool mint has got to be good in my book. The "double chocolate" comes into play with the chocolate filling and the flaky chocolaty crust.

Serves 8

1 parbaked Flaky Chocolate Crust (page 122), cooled
1¾ cups granulated sugar
½ cup Dutch-processed cocoa powder
2 tablespoons unbleached all-purpose flour
1 tablespoon yellow cornmeal
¼ teaspoon fine sea salt
5 large eggs
½ cup whole milk
4 tablespoons unsalted butter, melted
1 teaspoon pure vanilla extract
½ teaspoon mint extract

Position a rack in the middle of the oven and preheat the oven to 325°F. Put the baked pie shell on a baking sheet.

In a large mixing bowl, whisk together the sugar, cocoa powder, flour, cornmeal, and salt. Set aside.

In a medium bowl, whisk together the eggs, milk, butter, vanilla, and mint extract until smooth. Whisk the wet mixture into the dry mixture until completely incorporated. Pour the filling into the prepared piecrust.

Bake the pie for 35 to 40 minutes, until the filling is puffed up at the edges and the center no longer looks wet but still wobbles slightly; it will continue to set as it cools. Remove the pie from the oven and cool on a wire rack for 2 to 3 hours.

Serve the pie at room temperature or chilled.

The pie is best served the same day, but it can be refrigerated overnight.

BANOFFEE PIE

Serves 8

This pie has a rich layer of caramelized milk, which you can make in the oven or in a slow cooker. To use a slow cooker, take the paper wrapper off the can of condensed milk and place it in your slow cooker. Cover the can by at least 2 inches of water. Turn to low and cook for 5 hours. Cook more than one at a time, so when the mood strikes, you can just pull a can of cooked milk out of the refrigerator; it will keep for 1 month refrigerated.

One 14-ounce can sweetened condensed milk

1 prebaked Pecan–Graham Cracker Crust (page 117), cooled
2 large bananas
1½ cups heavy cream

¼ cup sour cream
¼ cup confectioners' sugar
2 ounces good-quality semisweet chocolate

Position a rack in the lower third of the oven and preheat the oven to 425°F.

Pour the sweetened condensed milk into a shallow baking dish. Cover the dish snugly with aluminum foil. Set the dish in a large roasting pan and add enough hot water to the roasting pan to reach halfway up the sides of the baking dish. Or use a slow cooker (see headnote).

Bake the milk for 40 minutes. Carefully remove the pans from the oven and give the milk a quick stir. Add more water to the roasting pan if needed and cook for another 30 to 35 minutes, until the milk turns a dark caramel color (see Tip).

Carefully remove the pans from the oven and whisk the milk until smooth; it will continue to thicken as it cools. Let cool to room temperature, about 30 minutes.

Pour the milk into the prepared piecrust. Cover with plastic wrap and refrigerate for at least 1 hour.

Once the pie has chilled, slice the bananas and arrange them on top.

In the bowl of a stand mixer fitted with the whisk attachment (or in a large mixing bowl, using a handheld mixer), whip the heavy cream and sour cream on medium speed until the cream starts to thicken. Add the confectioners' sugar and beat until the cream holds soft peaks. Spread the cream over the bananas and refrigerate the pie until ready to serve. The pie can be refrigerated for 2 days.

Just before serving, grate the chocolate on top of the whipped cream.

APPLE CUSTARD PIE

Serves 8

A touch of cardamom, lavender, and lemon zest brings a fresh flavor combination to this apple pie. I like to mix apples like Honeycrisp, Pink Ladys, and Granny Smith to give the pie an even more complex flavor.

1 prebaked Shortcut Piecrust (page 116), cooled

1 pound apples (see the headnote), peeled, cored, and thinly sliced

¼ cup packed light brown sugar

10 tablespoons (1¼ sticks) unsalted butter, melted

½ teaspoon ground cardamom

½ teaspoon food-grade dried lavender

2 teaspoons grated lemon zest

3 large eggs

1 cup whole milk

2 teaspoons pure vanilla extract

2 tablespoons unbleached all-purpose flour

⅓ cup granulated sugar

½ teaspoon fine sea salt

1 recipe Fresh Whipped Cream (page 61)

Position a rack in the middle of the oven and preheat the oven to 350°F. Put the baked pie shell on a baking sheet.

In a large saucepan, combine the apples, brown sugar, ¼ cup of the melted butter, the cardamom, lavender, and lemon zest and cook over medium heat, stirring, until the apples are tender, 3 to 5 minutes. Set aside to cool to room temperature.

In a medium bowl, whisk together the eggs, milk, the remaining melted butter, the vanilla, flour, granulated sugar, and salt. Pour half of the batter into the prebaked crust. Spoon the apples, with their juices, on top. Pour the remaining batter over the apples.

Bake for 25 to 30 minutes, until the filling is golden and puffed up at the edges and the center no longer looks wet but still wobbles slightly; it will continue to set as it cools. Remove the pie from the oven and cool on a wire rack for 2 to 3 hours.

Pile big mounds of whipped cream over the surface of the pie. Serve the pie chilled. It can be refrigerated for up to 2 days.

KEY LIME PIE

Serves 8

We start baking our classic key lime pie around Saint Patrick's Day, which is a *huge* celebration day in Savannah. The pie has a pleasing *almost* green hue, and the fresh taste is a great reminder that winter is almost over and summer will be here in the blink of an eye. Serve a big dollop of whipped cream on every slice.

1 prebaked Pecan–Graham Cracker Crust (page 117), cooled

One 14-ounce can sweetened condensed milk

½ cup heavy cream

½ teaspoon pure vanilla extract

3 large egg yolks

1 teaspoon grated lime zest

½ cup fresh key lime juice

1 recipe Fresh Whipped Cream (page 61)

Position a rack in the middle of the oven and preheat the oven to 325°F. Place the baked pie shell on a baking sheet.

In a large bowl, whisk together the condensed milk, heavy cream, vanilla, and egg yolks until smooth. Add the lime zest and lime juice and whisk until combined.

Pour the filling into the crust. Bake for 18 to 20 minutes, until the filling is puffed up at the edges and the center no longer looks wet but still wobbles slightly; it will continue to set as it cools.

Cool the pie on a wire rack for 1 hour, then refrigerate until cold.

Serve the pie chilled with the whipped cream. It can be refrigerated for up to 3 days.

ORANGE BUTTERMILK PIE

Serves 8

I created this pie in the middle of the winter, when clementines and satsuma oranges are in season. The flavor is simple and pure, and you can use any oranges that you like. Buttermilk is the key ingredient, so use the good stuff you can sometimes find in farmers' markets if possible. I count on the old-fashioned buttermilk that we get from our friends at Southern Swiss Dairy to give this pie the old-timey flavor I recall from childhood.

1 prebaked Shortcut Piecrust (page 116), cooled
6 tablespoons unsalted butter, at room temperature
1 cup granulated sugar
2 large eggs, separated

3 tablespoons unbleached all-purpose flour
1 teaspoon grated orange zest
2 tablespoons fresh orange juice
¼ teaspoon fine sea salt
1 cup buttermilk, at room temperature

1 recipe Fresh Whipped Cream (page 61)
Orange segments for garnish (optional)

Position a rack in the middle of the oven and preheat the oven to 325°F. Place the baked pie shell on a baking sheet.

In the bowl of a stand mixer fitted with the paddle attachment (or in a large mixing bowl, using a handheld mixer), cream the butter and sugar for 3 to 5 minutes, until light and fluffy. Add the egg yolks and mix well to combine. Add the flour, orange zest, orange juice, and salt and mix until well blended. With the mixer on low, slowly add the buttermilk, scraping down the sides of the bowl with a rubber spatula as needed. The mixture will look curdled at this point, but don't worry. If using a stand mixer, transfer to a large bowl. Set aside.

In the clean mixer bowl, using the whisk attachment (or in a medium mixing bowl, using clean beaters), beat the egg whites until soft peaks form. Give the buttermilk mixture a quick stir just to make sure that it is well blended, then add a small amount of the egg whites and fold in. Gently fold in the remaining egg whites until completely incorporated.

Pour the filling into the baked piecrust. Bake for 45 to 55 minutes, until the filling is golden and puffed up at the edges and the center no longer looks wet but still wobbles slightly; it will continue to set as it cools. Remove the pie from the oven and cool on a wire rack for 2 to 3 hours.

Serve the pie at room temperature or chilled, with the whipped cream. Garnish with segments of orange, if you'd like. The pie can be stored at room temperature for up to 1 day or refrigerated for up to 2 days.

GEORGIA PEACH PIE

Serves 8

In the middle of summer, fresh Georgia peaches are always on my mind. It's difficult to miss peaches at that time of year—they are abundant in big baskets in roadside stands all over Savannah. This juicy peach pie is the easiest recipe I can think of when I want a peach fix. But no matter how hard I try, I just can't wait for it to cool—I like a warm slice with vanilla bean ice cream.

1 recipe Extra-Flaky Piecrust (page 120)
2½ pounds peaches, peeled, pitted, and cut into ¼-inch slices
2 teaspoons grated lemon zest

2 tablespoons fresh lemon juice
¼ cup packed light brown sugar
3 tablespoons cornstarch
½ teaspoon fine sea salt
¼ teaspoon ground cinnamon

¼ teaspoon ground allspice
¼ teaspoon ground ginger

1 large egg, lightly beaten with a pinch of fine sea salt for egg wash
Coarse sugar or raw sugar for sprinkling

Roll out one disk of dough, fit it into a 9-inch pie pan, and refrigerate for 30 minutes, then "dock" the bottom of the crust and return it to the refrigerator (see How to Roll Out the Perfect Piecrust, page 118). Roll out the second disk, cut into lattice strips (see page 119), place on a baking sheet, and refrigerate.

Put the peaches in a large bowl, add the lemon zest and lemon juice, and toss gently.

In a small bowl, mix together the brown sugar, cornstarch, salt, cinnamon, allspice, and ginger. Gently toss the peaches with this mixture.

Pour the filling into the prepared piecrust. Use the chilled dough strips to form a lattice over the filling crust (see page 119). Put the pie on a baking sheet and put in the refrigerator for 15 minutes to set the crust.

Meanwhile, position a rack in the lower third of the oven and preheat the oven to 400°F.

Remove the pie from the refrigerator and brush the piecrust with the egg wash. Sprinkle with coarse sugar. Bake for 15 minutes, then reduce the oven temperature to 350°F and bake for 45 to 50 minutes, until the crust is golden brown and the fruit is bubbling. Remove the pie from the oven and cool on a wire rack for 2 to 3 hours.

The pie can be stored at room temperature for up to 1 day or refrigerated for up to 2 days.

BUTTERSCOTCH PIE

Serves 8

We found this recipe in Grandma Hannah's old recipe box, and it's a keeper. A smooth butterscotch pudding is tucked into a buttery crust and then topped with a brown sugar meringue, which gives the pie a delightful twist and a light caramel flavor.

6 large egg yolks
2 cups packed light brown sugar
½ cup unbleached all-purpose flour
3 tablespoons cornstarch
1 teaspoon fine sea salt
2¼ cups whole milk
8 tablespoons (1 stick) unsalted butter, at room temperature

1½ teaspoons pure vanilla extract
1 prebaked Shortcut Piecrust (page 116), cooled

FOR THE BROWN SUGAR MERINGUE
1½ cups packed light brown sugar
½ cup water

6 large egg whites
½ teaspoon cream of tartar
1 teaspoon pure vanilla extract

SPECIAL EQUIPMENT
Candy thermometer
Kitchen blowtorch

In a small bowl, lightly whisk the egg yolks. Set aside.

In a medium heavy saucepan, whisk together the brown sugar, flour, cornstarch, and salt. Set the pan over medium heat and gradually add the milk. Continue stirring until slightly thickened, 10 to 12 minutes.

Add about ½ cup of the warm milk mixture to the egg yolks to temper them, whisking vigorously so that the yolks do not curdle, then pour the egg yolk mixture into the rest of the milk mixture. Cook over medium heat, stirring frequently, until the filling is thickened, 6 to 8 minutes. Remove from the heat and fold in the butter and vanilla until the butter is melted and fully incorporated.

Transfer the filling to a heatproof bowl and place a piece of plastic wrap directly on top of the filling so that a skin does not form. Let cool for 30 minutes, or until it reaches room temperature. Place in the refrigerator for at least 2 hours to set. Pour the cooled filling into the prebaked piecrust. Cover the pie with plastic wrap and place it in the refrigerator to chill while you prepare the meringue topping.

To make the brown sugar meringue: In a small saucepan, combine the brown sugar and water and cook over medium heat, stirring occasionally, until the sugar has dissolved. Brush down the sides of the saucepan with a pastry brush dipped in warm water to remove any sugar crystals on the sides of the pan, then do not stir again. Clip a candy thermometer to the side of the saucepan and cook over medium heat until the syrup reaches 248°F (the "soft ball stage"), 8 to 10 minutes. Keep a constant eye on the thermometer; timing is very important here.

Meanwhile, combine the egg whites and cream of tartar in the bowl of a stand mixer fitted with the whisk attachment (or use a large mixing bowl and a handheld mixer) and beat until the whites hold soft peaks. Turn the mixer off.

As soon as the sugar syrup reaches 240°F, carefully lift the pan from the heat (use an oven mitt) and, with the mixer running on low, carefully pour the hot syrup into the egg white mixture in a slow, steady stream, avoiding the spinning whisk. Be careful: the syrup is very hot, and you don't want it to splash! Once all of the syrup is added, add the vanilla, raise the speed to high, and beat until the meringue has cooled to room temperature, 5 to 7 minutes. It will be very glossy and hold stiff peaks.

Spoon mounds of the meringue all over the surface of the chilled pie, then create big luscious swirls using a spatula or the back of a spoon. Toast the topping lightly with a kitchen blowtorch. Chill the pie before serving.

The pie can be refrigerated for up to 2 days.

BLACKBERRY AND APPLE PIE

• Serves 8 •

We are lucky enough to have access to delicious apples from northern Georgia, where the apples are so juicy you need to hold a napkin in one hand while you eat with the other. I like to mix assorted varieties, with tart and sweet flavors, such as Honeycrisp, Empire, and Rome Beauty. Choose the local apples you like best; most any variety will pair well with plump fresh blackberries.

1 recipe Extra-Flaky
   Piecrust (page 120)
2½ cups blackberries
2 teaspoons grated lemon
   zest
1 teaspoon fresh lemon
   juice
½ cup granulated sugar

2 tablespoons cornstarch
¼ teaspoon fine sea salt
¼ teaspoon ground
   cardamom
2½ pounds apples (see
   the headnote), cored,
   peeled, and sliced ½ inch
   thick

1 large egg, lightly beaten
   with a pinch of fine sea
   salt for egg wash
Coarse sugar or raw sugar
   for sprinkling

Roll out one disk of dough, fit it into a 9-inch pie pan, and refrigerate for 30 minutes, then "dock" the bottom of the crust and return it to the refrigerator (see How to Roll Out the Perfect Piecrust, page 118). Roll out the second disk to a 12-inch circle, place on a baking sheet, and refrigerate.

Position a rack in the lower third of the oven and preheat the oven to 400°F.

Put the blackberries in a large bowl, add the lemon zest and lemon juice, and toss gently. Transfer 1 cup of the blackberries to a small bowl and coarsely mash them with a fork, then mix them back in with the whole berries. Set aside for about 15 minutes.

In a small bowl, mix together the granulated sugar, cornstarch, salt, and cardamom. Gently toss the apples with the blackberries, then toss the fruit with the sugar mixture.

To assemble the pie: Pour the fruit filling into the crust. Brush half of the egg wash over the edges of the bottom crust. Place the top crust over the filling and press the edges together to seal. With kitchen shears, trim the crust to ½ inch from the edges of the pie pan. Leave it uncrimped to show off the flaky layers of the crust once baked. Place the pie in the refrigerator to chill for 15 minutes.

Remove the pie from the refrigerator and brush the top crust with the remaining egg wash and sprinkle with coarse sugar. Cut slits in the top of the crust. Bake for 15 minutes, then reduce the oven to 375°F and bake for an additional 45 to 50 minutes, until the crust is golden brown and the fruit is bubbling. Cool on a wire rack, 2 to 3 hours. The pie can be refrigerated for up to 2 days.

NECTARINE AND BLUEBERRY SLAB PIE

Serves 12

I love the combination of nectarines and blueberries. Nectarines have a taste similar to that of peaches, but since they don't have that fuzzy skin, you don't even have to peel them. You can also use any of your favorite seasonal fruits, such as strawberries and rhubarb, in this pie. It is a great dessert to take to a Saturday night supper club or make whenever you have to feed a crowd.

1 recipe Slab Piecrust (recipe follows)
5 cups sliced (½-inch wedges) nectarines
4 cups blueberries
1 cup granulated sugar
3 tablespoons cornstarch
½ teaspoon fine sea salt

1 tablespoon grated lemon zest
1 tablespoon fresh lemon juice

1 large egg, lightly beaten with a pinch of fine sea salt for egg wash

Raw sugar for sprinkling

SPECIAL EQUIPMENT
15-by-10-inch jelly-roll pan
Mini cookie cutters (optional)

On a lightly floured work surface, with a lightly floured rolling pin, roll the larger piece of dough into a 19-by-14-inch rectangle. Fit it into a 15-by-10-inch jelly-roll pan, pressing it into the corners; the crust will hang over the edges of the pan. Put the crust in the refrigerator to chill while you put the filling together.

Combine the nectarines and blueberries in a large bowl. Add the granulated sugar, cornstarch, salt, lemon zest, and lemon juice and toss with the fruit until thoroughly mixed. Pour the filling into the prepared crust.

On a lightly floured work surface, with a lightly floured rolling pin, roll out the smaller piece of dough into a 15-by-10-inch rectangle. Place it over the filling. Fold the edges of the bottom crust up over the top crust and pinch the edges to seal. Cut out shapes from the leftover dough with mini cutters, if desired, and use them to decorate the top of the pie. Chill the pie for 15 to 20 minutes to set the crust.

Meanwhile, position a rack in the middle of the oven and preheat the oven to 375°F.

Remove the pie from the refrigerator and cut a few slits in the top of the chilled crust to vent it. Brush the crust with the egg wash and sprinkle with raw sugar.

Bake for 40 to 55 minutes, until the crust is golden brown and the juices are bubbling. Remove the pie from the oven and cool on a wire rack, 2 to 3 hours.

Cut the pie into big squares and serve at room temperature or chilled.

The pie can be stored at room temperature for up to 1 day or refrigerated for up to 2 days.

SLAB PIECRUST | *Makes enough for one 15-by-10-inch slab pie*

3¾ cups unbleached all-purpose flour
1½ teaspoons granulated sugar
1 teaspoon fine sea salt
½ cup ice water
1 tablespoon cider vinegar
¾ pound (3 sticks) cold unsalted butter, cut into cubes

In a medium bowl, whisk together the flour, sugar, and salt. Set aside.

In a measuring cup or a small bowl, combine the water and cider vinegar. Set aside.

Toss the butter in the flour mixture to lightly coat it. Then, using a pastry blender, cut the butter into the flour. You should have various-sized pieces of butter, ranging from sandy patches to pea-sized chunks, with some larger bits as well. Drizzle in about half of the ice water mixture and stir lightly with a fork until the flour is moistened. If the dough seems dry, add more of the ice water, 1 to 2 tablespoons at a time. The dough will still look a bit shaggy at this point. If you grab a small piece and press it slightly with your hand, it should mostly hold together.

Dump the dough out onto an unfloured work surface and gather it together into a tight mound. Using the heel of your hand, smear the dough a little at a time, pushing away from you and working your way down the mass to create flat layers of flour and butter. Then gather the dough back together with a bench scraper, layering the clumps of dough on top of one another. Repeat the process once or twice more; the dough should still have some big pieces of butter visible.

Cut the dough into two pieces, one slightly larger than the other. Shape each piece into a disk and flatten them. Wrap the disks in plastic and put in the refrigerator for at least 1 hour, or overnight, to rest.

The dough can be stored for up to 3 days in the refrigerator or up to 1 month in the freezer. If frozen, defrost in the refrigerator overnight.

CHERRY POTPIE

Makes 8 potpies

Is there anything better than a potpie? What about a sweet potpie? Deep-dish and delicious, and covered with a flaky, buttery crust, these cute little pies are loaded with the flavor of cherries, brown sugar, and cardamom. Bake them in ramekins for a night in at home, or make them in Mason jars and pack them for a picnic in the park.

1 recipe Extra-Flaky
    Piecrust (page 120)
5 cups sweet cherries, pitted
1 tablespoon fresh lemon
    juice
¾ cup packed light brown
    sugar
3 tablespoons cornstarch

½ teaspoon fine sea salt
¼ teaspoon ground
    cardamom

1 large egg, lightly beaten
    with a pinch of fine sea
    salt for egg wash

SPECIAL EQUIPMENT
Eight 1-cup ramekins or
    widemouthed ½-pint
    oven-safe Mason jars

Dust your rolling pin with flour. Pull the 2 disks of dough out of the fridge and place each one on a lightly floured piece of parchment. Roll each into a circle about ⅛ inch thick. Then, using the top of a ramekin or the ring of a Mason jar lid as a guide, cut out 8 rounds of dough. Cut a small round hole in the center of each one or cut 3 slits to vent the steam. Cut out shapes from the dough scraps to decorate the crusts, if desired. Put the rounds on a baking sheet and place in the refrigerator to chill while you make the filling.

Put the cherries in a medium bowl, add the lemon juice, brown sugar, cornstarch, salt, and cardamom, and toss together until the cherries are evenly coated.

Line a baking sheet with parchment (to catch any drips). Place the ramekins or jars on the prepared baking sheet. Fill each one with about ½ cup filling. Top each one with a dough round. Gently press on the dough with your fingers or a fork to seal each top in place. Chill the pies in the refrigerator for 15 to 20 minutes to set the crust.

Position a rack in the lower third of the oven and preheat the oven to 375°F.

Remove the pies from the refrigerator and brush the crusts with the egg wash. Bake the potpies for 45 minutes, or until the crust is golden and the filling is bubbly. Remove the pies from the oven and cool on a wire rack for at least 30 minutes.

Serve the pies slightly warm, at room temperature, or chilled.

The pies can be stored at room temperature for up to 1 day or refrigerated for up to 2 days.

STRAWBERRY TART

Serves 8

I hoard strawberries when they're in season. I love to make them into jams and syrups to freeze, so I can pull them out on a cold, dreary winter's day to remind me of summer. This custard tart is topped with beautiful fresh strawberries in all their glory and then glazed with strawberry (or apricot) preserves.

5 large egg yolks
6 tablespoons granulated sugar
3 tablespoons cornstarch
¼ teaspoon fine sea salt
2 cups whole milk
1 teaspoon pure vanilla extract

2½ tablespoons unsalted butter, cut into cubes, at room temperature
1 prebaked Pecan–Graham Cracker Crust (page 117; shown in the photo) or Shortcut Piecrust (page 116), cooled

¼ cup strawberry or apricot preserves
2 pounds strawberries, hulled and sliced in half

1 recipe Fresh Whipped Cream (page 61)

In a heatproof bowl, whisk together the egg yolks, sugar, cornstarch, and salt until thick and pale in color.

In a medium saucepan, heat the milk to a gentle boil. Gradually add about 1 cup of the hot milk into the egg yolk mixture to temper the yolks, whisking constantly so they don't curdle, then whisk in the remainder of the milk in a steady stream.

Set the bowl over a saucepan of simmering water (do not let the bottom of the bowl touch the water) and cook, whisking constantly, until thickened, 5 to 7 minutes. Remove from the heat and whisk in the vanilla. Let the custard sit for 2 to 3 minutes to cool slightly, then gently whisk in the butter until it is melted and the custard is smooth and silky.

Place a piece of plastic wrap directly on top of the custard so that a skin does not form and let cool for 30 minutes, or until it reaches room temperature.

Spoon the cooled filling into the prepared piecrust. Cover with plastic wrap and place it in the refrigerator to chill for at least 3 hours, or overnight.

To finish the tart, in a small saucepan, heat the preserves over low heat, stirring, until liquefied and smooth. Set aside to cool.

Pile the strawberries on top of the custard filling. Brush the preserves all over the berries. Refrigerate until ready to serve, or for up to 2 days. Serve with whipped cream.

RAZZLEBERRY CRISP

Serves 8

Crisps are easy to whip up for a weekday dessert. I make this one with fresh fruit when it is in season, but the recipe also works if you have fruit put up for the winter in your larder or your freezer. The mint takes this crisp to another level of freshness.

FOR THE TOPPING

2 cups unbleached all-purpose flour

½ cup packed light brown sugar

1 teaspoon fine sea salt

2 tablespoons finely chopped fresh mint

12 tablespoons (1½ sticks) cold unsalted butter, cut into cubes

FOR THE FILLING

2 cups sliced strawberries

1 cup raspberries

1 cup blueberries

1 cup blackberries

1 Fuji or Gala apple, peeled, cored, and sliced

1 cup raw sugar

6 tablespoons unbleached all-purpose flour

¼ teaspoon fine sea salt

Position a rack in the middle of the oven and preheat the oven to 350°F. Butter a 9-inch deep-dish pie plate. Line a baking sheet with parchment.

To make the topping: In a medium mixing bowl, stir together the flour, brown sugar, salt, and mint with a fork until completely blended. Toss in the butter and work it in with your hands until it is the size of small peas. Put in the refrigerator to chill.

To make the filling: Put the strawberries, raspberries, blueberries, blackberries, and apple in a medium bowl. Whisk together the sugar, flour, and salt, add to the fruit, and gently toss together to coat the fruit.

Pour the fruit mixture into the prepared pie plate. Sprinkle the topping evenly over the fruit. Put the pie plate on the prepared baking sheet. Bake for 40 to 45 minutes, until the fruit is bubbling around the edges and the top is golden brown and crispy. Let cool slightly.

Serve the crisp warm. It is best eaten the same day, but it can be covered with plastic wrap once cooled and refrigerated for up to 3 days.

SHORTCUT PIECRUST

This is an easy-peasy piecrust that is simply pressed into the pan. It's buttery and flaky, yet no rolling is required.

Makes one 9-inch piecrust

1½ cups unbleached all-purpose flour

¼ cup packed light brown sugar

½ teaspoon fine sea salt

11 tablespoons unsalted butter, melted

In a medium bowl, whisk together the flour, sugar, and salt. Slowly drizzle in the butter and stir with a fork until the mixture looks evenly moist and crumbly.

Press the dough evenly over the bottom and up the sides of a 9-inch pie pan. You can crimp the edges decoratively with a fork or leave them as is. Put the crust in the freezer for about 15 minutes to set.

If the recipe calls for a parbaked or prebaked crust, preheat the oven to 375°F and follow the instructions on page 119. Let cool completely before filling.

PECAN-GRAHAM CRACKER CRUST

Our version of a simple graham cracker crust includes chopped Georgia pecans.

Makes one 9-inch piecrust

½ cup finely chopped pecans

2 cups graham cracker crumbs (about 16 crackers)

¼ cup packed light brown sugar

8 tablespoons (1 stick) unsalted butter, melted

Position a rack in the middle of the oven and preheat the oven to 350°F.

Spread the chopped pecans evenly on a baking sheet. Bake for 3 to 5 minutes, until lightly toasted. Set aside to cool.

In a medium bowl, mix together the graham cracker crumbs, pecans, and brown sugar. Drizzle in the butter a little at a time, mixing with a fork until the crumbs are evenly moistened.

Pour the crumb mixture over the bottom of a 9-inch pie pan and spread it out evenly. Using a flat-bottomed measuring cup, firmly press the crust into the bottom of the pan, working some of the crumbs up the sides of the pan. Put the crust in the freezer for about 15 minutes to set.

Bake the crust for 6 to 8 minutes, until lightly golden. Let cool completely before filling.

HOW TO ROLL OUT THE PERFECT PIECRUST

All piecrusts bake best when they have been chilled before baking. If you're refrigerating a piecrust for more than an hour, wrap it in plastic wrap to prevent your dough from drying out. Remove the chilled dough from the refrigerator 10 to 15 minutes before you want to roll it out.

Lightly dust your rolling pin with flour. Put the dough on a lightly floured surface, a pastry cloth, or parchment paper dusted with flour and dust the top of the dough with a little flour as well. Roll out the dough into a 12-inch round: Roll from the center out, rotating the dough as you roll to prevent sticking and to keep it as round as possible. Lightly dust the dough and work surface with flour again as necessary to prevent sticking. (You always want to roll dough until it is 1½ to 2 inches larger than the pie pan and about ⅛ inch in thickness.)

TROUBLESHOOTING

If the dough is too cold and cracks appear, let it warm up slightly and patch any cracks with small pieces of dough cut from the edges: Brush a little water onto the crust and press the patch onto the dough.

If the dough becomes too warm, you may see melting butter peeking through the crust. Chill it briefly, then dust it lightly with flour to seal and sweep the excess off using a pastry brush.

FITTING THE DOUGH INTO THE PIE PAN

Fold the dough in half and lay it across one side of a well-buttered pie pan, making sure the seam is in the center. Gently unfold the dough and carefully fit it into place. Trim the dough overhang to about 1½ inches.

Cover the crust with plastic wrap and chill in the refrigerator for at least 30 minutes. Flaky piecrusts always bake best when they have been chilled before baking. You can also refrigerate the crust at this point for up to 3 days or freeze it, well wrapped, for up to 1 month.

Once the crust is fully chilled, "dock" it—prick the bottom of the crust all over with a fork.

BAKING THE CRUST

If the recipe calls for a partially prebaked or "parbaked," or full prebaked crust, preheat the oven to 375°F.

Line the pie shell with parchment and fill with dried beans or pie weights. Bake for 10 minutes, or until the edges start to set. Remove the parchment and beans (they can be used again for baking, but not for eating!) and brush the bottom lightly with an egg-white wash (1 egg white, lightly beaten with a pinch of fine sea salt) to seal it and prevent sogginess.

For a parbaked crust, return the pan to the oven and bake for an additional 3 to 5 minutes, until the crust is lightly golden brown. Let cool completely before filling.

For a prebaked crust, bake for another 6 to 10 minutes, until the crust is golden brown. Let cool completely before filling.

HOW TO FINISH A SINGLE PIECRUST

Crimp the edges of the dough by using the index finger and thumb of one hand to create a letter C and pushing the thumb of your opposite hand against it, working your way all around the edges of the crust.

HOW TO FINISH A DOUBLE-CRUSTED PIE

Roll out the second disk of dough to a circle approximately 12 inches in diameter and about ⅛ inch thick. Place the top crust over the pie filling and pinch the top and bottom edges together to seal, then trim with kitchen shears, leaving a ½-inch overhang. You will be amazed at how this simple technique reveals the beautiful flaky layers of crust as it bakes.

Alternatively, you can crimp the edges of the crust as described above.

HOW TO MAKE A LATTICE CRUST

Roll out the second disk of dough to a circle approximately 12 inches in diameter and about ⅛ inch thick.

Using a pastry wheel, pizza cutter, or sharp knife, cut off a 1-inch-wide strip from two opposite sides of the circle. Cut the remaining dough into eight 1-inch-wide strips. Put the strips on a baking sheet and refrigerate until ready to use.

To make the lattice, starting with the longest strips, lay one strip across the center of the filled pie. Lay another strip across the middle of that strip (like a plus sign), then lay another strip perpendicular to that strip, about ½ inch away. Gently pull back one end of the bottom strip, lay another strip down perpendicular to it, and then put the strip back in place—it's like weaving. Repeat until you have used all of the strips and covered your pie.

To finish the edges, trim the lattice strips even with the bottom crust, then roll the bottom crust and lattice top inward all around the pie, creating a rolled edge. Make sure that the crust is resting on the edge of the pie plate. Then crimp the crust as directed above. Put the pie in the refrigerator to chill for 15 minutes to set the crust.

EXTRA-FLAKY PIECRUST

*Makes two
9-inch piecrusts
or 1 double
crust*

My grandmother taught me how to make pie dough. Her secret ingredient (aside from her loving touch) was a splash of cider vinegar. The vinegar helps relax the dough, which makes it easy to roll it out and fit it into the pan. This all-butter crust still amazes me every single time I make it. The various-sized chunks of butter melt as the dough bakes, leaving little voids that create layers and layers of flaky crust.

Making a piecrust from scratch takes a bit of courage, but once you've done it, you will never want to turn back. When making piecrust, practice makes perfect. As soon as you feel more comfortable, you will start making and freezing piecrusts, so that you can pull one out of your very own freezer (instead of the freezer at the grocery store!) when you're inspired to bake; see the Tip.

2½ cups unbleached all-purpose flour

1 tablespoon granulated sugar

1 teaspoon baking powder, preferably aluminum-free

1 teaspoon fine sea salt

½ cup ice water

1 tablespoon cider vinegar

½ pound (2 sticks) cold unsalted butter, cut into 1-inch cubes

In a medium bowl, whisk together the flour, sugar, baking powder, and salt. Set aside.

In a measuring cup or a small bowl, combine the water and cider vinegar. Set aside.

Toss the butter in the flour mixture to gently coat it. Then use a pastry blender to cut the butter into the flour. You should have various-sized pieces of butter, ranging from sandy patches to pea-sized chunks, with some larger bits as well. Drizzle in about half of the ice water mixture and stir lightly with a fork until the flour is evenly moistened and the dough starts to come together. If the dough seems dry, add a little more ice water, 1 to 2 tablespoons at a time. The dough will still look a bit shaggy at this point. If you grab a small piece of dough and press it slightly with your hand, it should mostly hold together.

Dump the dough out onto an unfloured work surface and gather it together into a tight mound. Using the heel of your hand, smear the dough a little at a time, pushing it away from you and working your way down the mass of dough to create flat layers of flour and butter. Then gather the dough back together with a bench scraper, layering the clumps of dough on top of one another. Repeat the process once or twice more; the dough should still have some big pieces of butter visible.

Cut the dough in half. Shape each piece into a disk and flatten it. Wrap the disks in plastic and put in the refrigerator for at least 1 hour, or overnight, to rest.

The dough can be stored for 3 days in the refrigerator or up to 1 month in the freezer. If frozen, defrost in the refrigerator overnight.

If the recipe calls for a parbaked or prebaked pie shell, preheat the oven to 375°F and follow the instructions on page 119. Let cool completely before filling.

Tip: It's easy to make piecrust in advance to freeze. Roll out the dough on a piece of parchment paper, then carefully roll it up in the parchment. Write the date on the parchment and pop into the freezer to firm up, about 30 minutes. Then wrap the crust securely in plastic wrap. The dough can be frozen for 1 month. Defrost the dough in the refrigerator overnight or thaw it on the kitchen counter for about 30 minutes.

FLAKY CHOCOLATE CRUST

This is an old-fashioned flaky crust with a rich, decadent chocolate flavor. Pair it with any custard or chess pie, especially the Double-Chocolate Mint Chess Pie (page 94).

Makes one 9-inch piecrust

1 cup unbleached all-purpose flour
¼ cup Dutch-processed cocoa powder

1½ teaspoons granulated sugar
½ teaspoon fine sea salt
½ cup ice water

1 tablespoon cider vinegar
8 tablespoons (1 stick) cold unsalted butter, cut into 1-inch cubes

In a medium bowl, whisk together the flour, cocoa, sugar, and salt. Set aside.

In a measuring cup or a small bowl, combine the water and cider vinegar. Set aside.

Toss the butter into the flour mixture to gently coat it. Then use a pastry blender to cut the butter into the flour. You should have various-sized pieces of butter, ranging from sandy patches to pea-sized chunks, with some larger bits as well. Add about half of the ice water mixture and stir lightly with a fork until the flour is evenly moistened and the dough begins to come together into a ball. If the dough seems dry, add a little more ice water, 1 to 2 tablespoons at a time.

Gather the dough together and flatten it into a disk. Wrap it in plastic and put in the refrigerator for at least 1 hour, or overnight, to rest.

The dough can be stored for up to 3 days in the refrigerator or up to 1 month in the freezer. If frozen, defrost in the refrigerator overnight.

If the recipe calls for a parbaked or prebaked pie shell, preheat the oven to 375°F and follow the instructions on page 119. Let cool completely before filling.

BEST-IN-SHOW PIE BANNER

I have always been drawn to the ornate beauty of vintage prize ribbons—the kind you would find at a state fair—so much so that I like to make a best-in-show banner for anything from a game night to a pie-making contest. Having people over for a weekend barbecue and a pie contest is a great way to encourage a little friendly competition. At the end of the night, everyone leaves happy, some with leftovers and at least one with bragging rights because he or she won the best-of banner of the night. *Makes 1 banner*

MATERIALS

An 18-inch length of fabric in the color or pattern of your choice

Iron-on adhesive, such as Heat & Bond

2 to 3 pieces printer paper

Felt in two contrasting colors

Fabric glue

Dowel rod

2 wooden beads

String

TOOLS

Scissors

Iron

Printer

Step 1: Cut a pennant out of the fabric. Fold over the edges and press with a hot iron. Apply iron-on adhesive to secure the folded edges and press with the hot iron again.

Step 2: Print out the words "BEST PIE" (or whatever words you'd like) to fit the size of your pennant onto printer paper.

Step 3: Using your printed letters as a template, cut out two sets of letters, one from each piece of felt. Stack the two colors of felt for each letter and attach to the pennant using fabric glue.

Step 4: Fold the top of the pennant over to create a channel for the dowel to slip through, glue it to secure, and allow to dry.

Step 5: Slip the dowel through the channel. Glue a wooden bead to each end of the dowel.

Step 6: Attach the string to each end of the dowel. Your pennant is ready to hang. Your guests' eyes are guaranteed to be on this prize!

YOUR DAY-LY BREAD

BREADS, ROLLS, AND CRACKERS

Griff begins his mornings at the bakery with a pot of coffee brewing and the baking list of what needs to be done for the day, which always includes mixing the bread doughs.

Scaling (i.e., measuring) the ingredients and prepping the big bread mixer for the first batch of dough are part of the daily ritual. I'm at the bakery by the time the mixer starts, and I hear the low whirring of the motor as it turns round and round. It takes only a short mix before Griff is dumping the dough into bins, hand-folding it, and then keeping a close eye on the proofing and the gentle rise that happens over time.

Bread is fascinating. It amazes me to think how the simplest of ingredients—flour, water, salt, and yeast—can be transformed into one of my absolute favorite foods. I am a happy girl eating a simple slice of one of Griff's breads, toasted and buttered.

There is really no need to be intimidated by the thought of making bread at home. Griff says knowledge and technique are the keys to making good bread; I'd say time and patience are keys too. Once you start making bread, your confidence will build and your overall understanding of baking will increase, bringing it to a new level. You'll see how time, temperature, and technique come together as one when you're making bread in the same way they do when you make a cake or bake your favorite cookies.

Lunch service has become a major part of our business. We opened the bakery with sweets and coffee, and eventually it seemed like a natural transition to develop a lunch menu too. Griff's obsession with creating yummy sandwiches is a popular draw for our customers. I think he just wants to make sure his favorite breads are put to good use! For us, a great sandwich is built around the bread, whether it's the classic Honey White Bread (page 128), Sorghum Whole Wheat Bread (page 131), or Cornmeal Sandwich Buns (page 135). The bread should always complement the ingredients inside and make everything come together. Here we share our favorite sandwich ideas, such as our Thanksgiving Sandwich (page 144) and Pimento and Pig Sandwich (page 144), along with the condiments (such as Sweet Potato Comeback Sauce, page 273) that have become favorites at the bakery, but I encourage you to take some of these and make them your own. If you find yourself with some time during your week, make the Rosemary Focaccia (page 132). Save the more advanced Ciabatta Rolls (page 138) for the weekend—it's a two-day project, but you will be so glad you tried it. And when you make your own bread at home, I'm certain you'll be inspired with countless ways to use it.

HONEY WHITE BREAD

*Makes
2 loaves*

Honey white is the loaf that started Griff on his journey of bread making. You can start your bread making with this recipe too; it's easy and quick, with just a few simple ingredients. This recipe will satisfy your hunger for fresh bread in just a few hours. Because bakers love to share, it makes two loaves.

5½ cups unbleached all-purpose flour
1 tablespoon fine sea salt
1 teaspoon granulated sugar
1½ teaspoons instant yeast

8 tablespoons (1 stick) unsalted butter, melted and cooled
2 large eggs, lightly beaten
1 cup whole milk, at room temperature
1½ tablespoons honey

¾ cup room-temperature water

1 large egg, lightly beaten with a pinch of fine sea salt for egg wash

In the bowl of a stand mixer fitted with the dough hook, combine the flour, salt, sugar, and instant yeast. Add the melted butter, eggs, milk, honey, and water, turn the mixer on low speed, and mix for 3 to 5 minutes, scraping the sides of the bowl occasionally, until the dough comes together in a shaggy mass. Turn the speed up to medium and mix for a full 7 minutes. The dough will begin to rise up on the dough hook but will still stick to the bottom of the bowl.

Transfer the dough to a lightly floured work surface and knead for 30 to 60 seconds, until smooth and elastic. Shape the dough into a ball.

Butter a large bowl and put the dough in the bowl, turning to coat it. Cover the bowl with plastic wrap and put in a warm, draft-free area. Let the dough rise for 1 hour, or until doubled in size.

Grease two 9-by-5-inch loaf pans with butter. Divide the dough into 2 equal parts. Using a rolling pin, roll each piece into an 8-by-10-inch rectangle. Starting from a short side, roll each piece up into a log and place seam side down in the bread pans. Loosely cover each pan with plastic wrap and allow the dough to rise for another hour, or until doubled in size.

Meanwhile, position a rack in the middle of the oven and preheat the oven to 350°F.

Brush the tops of the loaves with the egg wash. Bake for 40 to 45 minutes; the interior temperature should read 190°F on an instant-read thermometer and the crust should look like dark honey.

Remove the breads from the pans and place on a wire rack to cool.

The bread can be stored in an airtight container for up to 2 days.

SORGHUM WHOLE WHEAT BREAD

Makes 1 loaf

By the 1890s, sorghum was established in the South as a sweetener with beneficial nutrients. These days, corn syrup may be cheaper, but many in the South still use sorghum. Its deep caramel fruity flavor is unmatched by any honey or molasses.

3½ cups whole wheat flour
1 tablespoon instant yeast
1 tablespoon fine sea salt
¼ cup sorghum

¼ cup canola oil
½ cup whole milk
¾ cup room-temperature water

1 large egg, lightly beaten with a pinch of fine sea salt for egg wash

OPTIONAL SPECIAL EQUIPMENT
Instant-read thermometer

In the bowl of a stand mixer fitted with the dough hook, combine the flour, yeast, and salt. Add the sorghum, canola oil, milk, and water and blend on low speed for 3 minutes. Turn the mixer to medium speed and mix for 7 to 8 minutes. The dough should be soft yet firm to the touch.

Transfer the dough to a lightly floured work surface and knead and shape it into a ball. Transfer the dough to a lightly oiled bowl, turning to coat with oil. Cover with plastic wrap and put in a warm draft-free place. Allow the dough to rise for 2 hours, or until almost doubled in size.

Lightly spray a 9-by-5-inch loaf pan with nonstick spray. Transfer the dough to a lightly floured work surface and shape it into a rectangle, about 8 inches long by 6 inches wide. Starting with a long edge, gently roll the dough into a cylinder. Place the dough seam side down in the prepared loaf pan, cover with plastic wrap, and allow to rise for 1 hour, or until the dough rises about 1 inch above the edges of the pan. Brush with the egg wash.

Meanwhile, position an oven rack in the middle of the oven and preheat the oven to 350°F.

Place the loaf pan in the oven and bake for 30 to 35 minutes, until the bread is nicely browned; the center of the loaf should read 190°F on an instant-read thermometer. Remove the bread from the oven and place the pan on a wire rack for 2 minutes, then remove the bread from the pan and cool completely on the rack.

The bread can be stored in an airtight container for up to 5 days. To freeze, wrap the loaf in plastic wrap and then aluminum foil; it'll keep for up to 1 month.

ROSEMARY FOCACCIA

Makes 1 large bread

Focaccia is a great bread for everyday use. And making focaccia involves just a few basic steps—a quick mix by hand, one rise, and the bake—and it doesn't require a lot of prep time either. Slice a hunk in half to make a hearty sandwich or add torn pieces to a green salad.

5 cups unbleached all-purpose flour

¼ cup extra virgin olive oil, plus ¼ cup for the baking sheet

3 tablespoons granulated sugar

¾ cup grated Pecorino Romano

1 tablespoon instant yeast

1 tablespoon finely chopped fresh rosemary

1 teaspoon dried oregano

1 teaspoon coarsely ground black pepper

¾ teaspoon fine sea salt

2½ cups room-temperature water

2 teaspoons flaky sea salt, such as Jacobsen or Maldon

In the bowl of a stand mixer fitted with the dough hook, combine the flour, ¼ cup oil, the sugar, cheese, yeast, half the rosemary, the oregano, pepper, and salt and blend on low speed. With the mixer on low speed, add the water and mix for 3 minutes. Turn the mixer speed to medium-low and mix for 5 minutes.

Lightly coat a large bowl with nonstick spray. Transfer the dough into the bowl and cover with plastic wrap. Allow the dough to rise in a warm, draft-free place (about 70°F) for 1 to 1½ hours, until doubled in size.

At least 30 minutes before baking, position a rack in the middle of the oven and preheat the oven to 450°F. Line a 12-by-17-inch rimmed baking pan with parchment and brush with ¼ cup olive oil.

Transfer the dough to the oiled pan and turn to coat the dough with the oil, making sure the dough does not stick to the pan. Allow the dough to rest for 10 minutes, then coat your hands with oil and gently stretch and pull out the dough to the edges of the pan. Dimple the dough all over with your fingers and stretch the dough again if necessary to fill the pan. Allow the dough to rise for 30 to 60 minutes, until doubled in size.

Gently dimple the dough with oiled fingers again. Sprinkle the remaining rosemary over the top and finish with the flaky sea salt. Place in the oven, immediately reduce the oven temperature to 375°F, and bake for 20 to 30 minutes, until the bread is golden brown. Remove from the oven and transfer the bread to a wire rack to cool.

The focaccia can be stored in an airtight container for up to 2 days.

BUTTERMILK DINNER ROLLS

*Makes
24 rolls*

When I was growing up, the scent of freshly baked bread was a sign that Sunday dinner was almost ready. These soft, fragrant buttermilk rolls were always served with the meal, daubed with a little soft butter. I'd have to restrain myself from filling up on the rolls. If you can get fresh buttermilk from a local farm or farmers' market, use it here; it's far better than what you'll find in the grocery store. The buttermilk adds tenderness and just the right amount of tang to balance the sweet, delicate flavor of the rolls.

4 cups unbleached all-purpose flour
¼ cup granulated sugar
1 tablespoon instant yeast
2½ teaspoons fine sea salt

1½ cups buttermilk
5 tablespoons unsalted butter, at room temperature
2 teaspoons maple syrup

1 large egg, lightly beaten with a pinch of fine sea salt for egg wash

In the bowl of a stand mixer fitted with the dough hook, combine the flour, sugar, yeast, salt, buttermilk, butter, and syrup. Turn the speed to low and mix until blended, 2 to 3 minutes. Increase the speed to medium and mix for a full 7 minutes. The dough will come together but feel sticky; it will stick to the bottom of the bowl just a little bit.

Transfer the dough to a lightly floured work surface and knead a few times, until it is soft and supple, and form into a ball.

Lightly butter a large bowl. Put the dough in the bowl, turning to coat. Cover tightly with plastic wrap and let rise in a warm, draft-free place for 1½ to 2 hours, until doubled in size.

Lightly butter a baking sheet.

Transfer the dough to a lightly floured work surface. Use a bench scraper to divide the dough in half and then in half again, then cut each piece into 6 pieces so you have 24 pieces, about 1½ ounces each. Shape each one into a ball and place the balls about an inch apart in rows of 6 by 4 in the pan. Cover loosely with plastic wrap and let rise in a warm place for 1 hour, or until doubled in size.

Meanwhile, position a rack in the middle of the oven and preheat the oven to 375°F.

Remove the plastic wrap and gently brush each roll with the egg wash, making sure to cover the sides. Bake the rolls for 16 to 20 minutes, until nicely browned. Serve warm from the oven. The buttermilk rolls can be stored in an airtight container for up to 5 days.

CORNMEAL SANDWICH BUNS

*Makes
6 large
buns*

Grilling is one of our favorite things to do on summer weekends. We often start by making this easy dough (no mixer required) that bakes into tender, buttery buns. The buns are perfect with juicy hamburgers or pulled smoked pork, dripping in barbecue sauce. The cornmeal adds a lovely yellow hue, a touch of sweetness, and a bit of crunch for just the right texture.

¾ cup coarse yellow cornmeal

¾ cup boiling water

2 tablespoons unsalted butter, at room temperature

1 teaspoon honey

1 tablespoon sour cream, at room temperature

1¾ teaspoons fine sea salt

¾ cup room-temperature water

2¼ cups bread flour

¾ teaspoon instant yeast

1 large egg, lightly beaten with a pinch of fine sea salt for egg wash

1½ teaspoons sesame seeds or cornmeal (optional)

Put the ¾ cup cornmeal in a medium bowl and stir in the boiling water with a wooden spoon. Allow the cornmeal to stand until the water is absorbed, about 12 minutes.

Add the butter, honey, sour cream, salt, and room-temperature water to the cornmeal and stir to combine.

In a small bowl, stir together the flour and instant yeast, then stir into the cornmeal mixture. Using a wooden spoon, bowl scraper, or even your (clean!) hands, mix and fold the dough until smooth and soft; it will be sticky.

Transfer the dough to a large bowl, cover with plastic wrap, and allow to rest for 10 minutes.

Leaving the dough in the bowl, with lightly oiled hands, fold the edge farthest from you over toward the center. Then fold the bottom edge over toward the center, just as if you were folding a letter in thirds. Do the same fold again from the left side toward the center and then the right side. Cover with plastic wrap and allow the dough to rest for 10 minutes.

Do the same folding technique, but this time give the dough a little more stretch as you fold it top to bottom and side to side. Turn the dough seam side down, cover with plastic wrap, and allow it to rest for 10 minutes.

continued

Repeat the folding technique again, then turn the dough seam side down and cover the bowl tightly with plastic wrap. Put the bowl in a warm, draft-free place and let the dough rise until doubled in size, 45 to 60 minutes.

Transfer the dough to a lightly floured work surface. Using a rolling pin, roll the dough into an 8-by-10-inch rectangle, about 1 inch thick. Cut the dough into 6 equal pieces with a bench scraper or knife and form into balls.

Place the balls on a baking sheet, leaving 2 inches between them. Brush with the egg wash and top each bun with ¼ teaspoon sesame seeds or cornmeal, if using. Cover the pan with plastic wrap and allow the buns to rise in a warm, draft-free area for 1 hour, or until doubled in size.

At least 30 minutes before baking, position a rack in the middle of the oven and preheat the oven to 400°F.

Place the baking sheet in the oven and bake, rotating the pan halfway through, for 20 to 25 minutes, until the buns are a dark golden color. Remove the buns from the oven, transfer to a wire rack, and let cool completely.

The sandwich buns can be stored in an airtight container for up to 3 days. To freeze, wrap each bun in plastic wrap and place in a freezer bag; they will keep for up to 1 month.

CIABATTA ROLLS

*Makes
16 rolls*

Ciabatta is a soft Italian bread with a thin, chewy crust. It can be served as an everyday table bread or used for sandwiches. We use a pre-ferment, also known as a *poolish*, for this dough. Using a pre-ferment imparts great flavor and texture that is unmatched by using quicker conventional leavening. Ciabatta is simple enough for the beginning baker, but you will need two days to make it. Trust us—it's fun to make this dough, even though it may take longer and be a little stickier than what you are used to; see the techniques photos on pages 140–141.

FOR THE POOLISH

2¼ cups unbleached bread
    flour
⅛ teaspoon instant yeast
1¼ cups room-temperature
    water

FOR THE DOUGH

5 cups unbleached bread
    flour
2 tablespoons medium rye
    flour
1 tablespoon fine sea salt
1½ teaspoons instant yeast
1¾ cups plus 2 tablespoons
    room-temperature water

About 2 teaspoons olive oil
Coarse cornmeal for
    sprinkling

SPECIAL EQUIPMENT

Baking stone
Bread peel (optional)

To make the poolish: In a large bowl, whisk the flour and yeast to combine. Add the water and, using a plastic dough scraper, mix the ingredients until you have a shaggy mass. Cover with plastic wrap and let ferment overnight, 12 to 16 hours, at room temperature (approximately 70°F).

The next day, make the dough: In the bowl of a stand mixer fitted with the dough hook, combine the bread flour, rye flour, salt, yeast, poolish, and water and mix on the lowest speed for 3 minutes. Turn the mixer to medium speed and mix for 4 to 5 minutes. As the dough develops the gluten, it will start to pull away from the sides of the bowl, but it will still stick to the bottom of the bowl. It will be sticky to the touch, but if pulled on, it should have a firmness to it.

Oil a large bowl with olive oil. Transfer the dough to the bowl. Now you will start to fold the dough inside the bowl and then continue during a gentle rise of 3 hours; this builds the gluten and gives the dough strength. The dough will seem very loose and sticky at first, but as it rises, you will feel it becoming more manageable (it's fun to watch this dough rise). With lightly oiled (clean!) hands, fold the edge farthest from you toward the center. Fold the bottom edge over toward the center, just as if you were folding a letter in thirds. Do the same fold again, from the left side toward the center and then the right side over. Cover with plastic wrap, put the bowl in a warm draft-free place, and allow the dough to rise for 45 minutes.

Repeat the folding technique and allow the dough to rise for 45 minutes again, then repeat the process 2 more times.

After the final rise, invert the dough onto a heavily floured work surface. Using a bench scraper, divide the dough in half and then in half again, then cut each piece into 4 equal pieces. Gently shape each piece into a round shape, doing your best not to deflate the dough; you want to make sure the air and lightness of the dough remains. Lightly dust the tops of the rolls with flour, cover with plastic wrap, and let rise for 1 hour.

Meanwhile, as soon as you have shaped the dough, position a rack in the middle of the oven and place a baking stone on the rack. Preheat the oven to 450°F.

Sprinkle a bread peel or the back of a baking sheet lightly with coarse cornmeal. Transfer 8 rolls to the peel or pan, placing them side by side. With a gentle shaking motion, transfer the rolls to the baking stone.

Bake for 18 to 22 minutes, until the rolls are a dark amber color. Cover the remaining 8 rolls with plastic wrap while the first batch is baking. Transfer the rolls to a wire rack to cool completely, then repeat the loading and baking process with the remaining rolls.

The rolls can be stored in an airtight container for 1 day. To freeze, wrap each roll in plastic wrap and then aluminum foil; they will keep for up to 1 month.

Tip: Ciabatta dough is a soft, wet dough that may be difficult at first for beginning bread bakers to handle. But avoid the urge to add more flour during the mix—it'll make your bread tough.

HOW TO MAKE CIABATTA ROLLS

Ciabatta is a wonderful bread to learn how to make at home. Just be sure to plan in advance before you start. Once you become comfortable working with this wet and sticky dough, you will be rewarded with its aromatic flavor and a bread with a thin, crispy crust. This recipe introduces the use of a pre-ferment, which adds great flavor and structure to the dough, and once the dough is mixed, minimal effort is needed to create a wonderful loaf of bread or these fantastic rolls.

CIABATTA STEP-BY-STEP

MAKING THE POOLISH

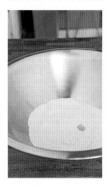

Put the flour and yeast into a large bowl and whisk until combined.

Add the water to the dry ingredients.

Using a plastic dough scraper, mix the ingredients until you have a shaggy mass.

Cover the bowl tightly with plastic wrap and allow to ferment overnight, 12 to 16 hours, at room temperature.

Combine both flours, the salt, yeast, poolish, and water in the mixer bowl.

Mix on low speed for 3 minutes, then mix on medium speed for 4 to 5 minutes, until the dough is firmer but still sticky.

Scrape the dough into a lightly oiled large bowl. Cover tightly with plastic wrap.

Fold the dough.

Allow the dough to rise, and repeat the folding process.

Transfer the dough to a floured surface and divide into 16 equal pieces.

Gently shape the dough into rounds and dust with flour before allowing to rise again and baking.

SWEET POTATO LEMON BREAD

Makes 2 loaves

This sweet potato loaf is nutritious and delicious all by itself, but it also makes a great base for a sandwich—see the Thanksgiving Sandwich on page 144. Baking the sweet potato before adding it to the dough brings out its natural sugars, making this an ideal breakfast bread; it's good for French toast too.

5½ cups unbleached all-purpose flour
½ cup packed light brown sugar
½ cup fine yellow cornmeal
1 tablespoon fine sea salt

2 teaspoons grated lemon zest
1½ teaspoons instant yeast
1 cup mashed baked sweet potato
2 large eggs

1¼ cups room-temperature water

1 large egg, lightly beaten with a pinch of fine sea salt for egg wash

OPTIONAL SPECIAL EQUIPMENT
Instant-read thermometer

In the bowl of a stand mixer fitted with the dough hook, combine the flour, sugar, cornmeal, salt, lemon zest, and instant yeast and mix to blend.

In a medium bowl, whisk the sweet potato and eggs to combine. Add to the flour mixture, turn the mixer on to low speed, add the water, and mix for 3 to 5 minutes, scraping the sides of the bowl as necessary, until the dough comes together. Turn the mixer speed to medium and mix for 7 minutes.

Transfer the dough to a lightly floured work surface and knead for about a minute, until smooth and elastic. Shape the dough into a ball.

Lightly butter a large bowl and put the dough in the bowl, turning it to coat. Cover the bowl with plastic wrap, put in a warm, draft-free place, and allow the dough to rise for 2 hours, or until doubled in size.

Grease two 9-by-5-inch loaf pans with butter.

Divide the dough into 2 equal pieces. Using a rolling pin, roll each piece into an 8-by-10-inch rectangle. Starting from a short side, roll each piece up into a log and place seam side down in the loaf pans. Loosely cover each pan with plastic wrap and allow the dough to rise until doubled in size, about 1 hour.

Meanwhile, position a rack in the middle of the oven and preheat the oven to 350°F.

Lightly brush the tops of the loaves with the egg wash. Bake the bread for 30 to 40 minutes, until the crust is the color of dark honey; the interior temperature should read 190°F on an instant-read thermometer. Remove the bread from the pans and place on a wire rack to cool.

The bread can be stored in an airtight container for up to 5 days. To freeze, wrap each loaf in plastic wrap and then aluminum foil; they will keep for up to 1 month.

MAKE GOOD
USE OF ALL
YOUR BREAD

At the bakery, our lunch menu has become one of the things our customers come back for day after day. Made to order on our fresh bread, our sandwiches reflect the season and fresh local ingredients. Here are a few of our favorites.

THANKSGIVING SANDWICH

We put this sandwich on our menu right after Thanksgiving. Use 2 slices of our Sweet Potato Lemon Bread (page 142), coated with Sweet Potato Comeback Sauce (page 273), and add a few slices of roasted turkey, sliced Swiss or cheddar cheese, sliced red onion and Roma tomatoes, and crispy Romaine lettuce leaves. Do a little turkey dance before enjoying the sandwich.

PIMENTO AND PIG SANDWICH

Our Pimento and Pig Panino is one of our top sellers. Grill up some thick-cut apple-smoked bacon. Slice a Ciabatta Roll (page 138), fill it with Pimento Cheese (page 221) and the bacon, and toast it in a panini press. With a bowl of tomato soup, one of these easily can be turned into a melty delicious meal.

SUPER CHICKEN SANDWICH

Prepare an herbed mayo: 2 cups mayonnaise mixed with 1 tablespoon herbes de Provence and ½ teaspoon fennel seeds. Split a Cornmeal Sandwich Bun (page 135), spread with the herbed mayo, and stuff with sliced roasted chicken breast, sliced sharp white cheddar cheese, red onion slices, beefsteak tomato slices, and a few leaves of tender Boston lettuce.

SAVORY ROSEMARY LEMON SHORTBREAD

This savory shortbread is an easy make-ahead recipe to serve at a party—or enjoy for weekday snacking. The flavor is a little salty and a bit spicy, so these go well with a plate of cheese and cured meats. The addition of rice cereal gives them a crispy bite.

Makes 48 crackers

½ pound (2 sticks) unsalted butter, at room temperature

2½ cups unbleached all-purpose flour

1 cup lightly packed finely grated Gruyère cheese

1 cup crispy rice cereal

2 teaspoons grated lemon zest

2 teaspoons fresh lemon juice

2 teaspoons chopped fresh rosemary

1 teaspoon freshly ground black pepper

½ teaspoon fine sea salt

In the bowl of a stand mixer fitted with the paddle attachment (or in a large mixing bowl, using a handheld mixer), cream the butter on medium speed until smooth, about 3 minutes. Add the flour, cheese, cereal, lemon zest, lemon juice, rosemary, pepper, and salt and mix on low until the dough comes together, then turn the speed to medium and mix until the dough is smooth, 2 to 3 minutes.

Transfer the dough to a lightly floured work surface and divide into 2 equal parts. Roll each piece of dough into a 12-inch-long log. Wrap in plastic wrap and place in the freezer for 30 minutes.

Position the racks in the middle and lower third of the oven and preheat the oven to 350°F. Line two baking sheets with parchment.

Remove the logs from the freezer. Cut each log into ½-inch-thick rounds and arrange about 1 inch apart on the prepared pans.

Bake for 20 to 22 minutes, until the crackers are lightly golden on the edges, rotating the pans halfway through the baking time. Cool completely.

The crackers can be stored in an airtight container for up to 2 weeks.

PIMENTO CHEESE CRACKERS

Makes about 120 crackers

A little time and effort goes a long way when you make your own crackers. Oh, sure, you can buy them in a box, but your family and friends will enjoy them even more when they know they are handmade. Use a good-quality cheddar here; the smoky paprika adds a kick of flavor.

1 pound sharp white cheddar cheese, shredded

8 tablespoons (1 stick) unsalted butter, at room temperature

1¼ teaspoons smoked paprika, plus more for dusting

1 teaspoon fine sea salt

¼ teaspoon cayenne pepper

¼ teaspoon balsamic vinegar

1½ cups unbleached all-purpose flour

Flaky sea salt, such as Jacobsen or Maldon, for sprinkling

In the bowl of a stand mixer fitted with the paddle attachment (or in a medium bowl, using a handheld mixer), combine the cheese, butter, paprika, fine sea salt, cayenne, and balsamic vinegar and mix on low speed until the ingredients come together. Increase the speed to medium-high and mix until smooth and well blended, 4 to 5 minutes.

Turn the mixer back to low and add the flour in thirds, scraping the sides and bottom of the bowl as necessary. Turn the speed to medium-high and mix for 30 to 60 seconds, until a soft dough forms.

Scrape the dough out of the bowl and divide into 2 equal pieces. Roll each piece into a 1½-by-9-inch log. Wrap each log in plastic wrap and refrigerate for 4 hours. (The dough can be refrigerated for up to 2 days or, wrapped in plastic wrap and then aluminum foil, frozen for up to 1 month.) If baking from frozen, thaw in the fridge.

Position the racks in the upper and lower thirds of the oven and preheat the oven to 350°F. Line two baking sheets with parchment.

Slice one log of dough into ⅛-inch-thick rounds and space them about ½ inch apart on the pans. Top the crackers with flaky sea salt and, using a fine-mesh sieve, dust the tops with smoked paprika.

Bake for 18 to 20 minutes, until the crackers are lightly browned, rotating the pans halfway through the baking time. Cool the pans on wire racks. The crackers can be stored in an airtight container for up to 1 week.

SNACK POCKET

Vintage linens are a part of my everyday world: I inherited quite a collection from all of the ladies in my family, and now my dear friend Haylie carries on the tradition by sending me packages of linens from her travels. Beautiful linens are very affordable at thrift stores and flea markets, as long as you are looking for "cutters," which are not in absolutely perfect condition. I constantly scoop them up not only to use on my dining table, but also to repurpose them. I like to wrap gifts, especially food gifts, with the linens. I often use them as impromptu aprons, too, especially when I have tiny chefs in the kitchen. This easy project shows how to reinvent a vintage napkin as a snack carrier. I pop one in my tote bag before I leave the house each morning. Make several to pack sandwiches for picnics in the park or to pack in your Lunch Canister (see page 226). *Makes 1 pocket*

MATERIALS
Square vintage napkin
Fabric dye (optional)
Thread

TOOLS
Iron
Straight pins
Needle

Step 1: Lay the napkin right side down, oriented like a diamond, on an ironing board. Fold the left and right corners over to meet in the center and press with a hot iron. Fold the bottom corner up, overlapping the edges by ⅛ to ¼ inch; the napkin should begin to resemble an envelope. Press into place and then pin to secure temporarily.

Step 2: Using a needle and thread, stitch the overlapping edges to secure the fabric. You can do a hidden stitch or use a simple embroidery technique, such as a cross-stitch or a running stitch.

Step 3: Fold the top corner of the napkin down to close the envelope. Press into place, and start using your new snack holder.

HOLIDAYS AND CELEBRATIONS

CUPCAKES, LAYER CAKES, AND OTHER SPECIAL-OCCASION SWEETS

I love holiday baking more than just about anything. Would you believe that I start thinking about our annual holiday bash in July? When it's someone's birthday, I like to refer to it as his or her "birthday season." I believe birthdays are major milestones that deserve more than just one day of celebration—don't you? And I admit I have been known to invent an occasion just to be able to mark it with a special dessert. Luckily for me, holidays happen for us year-round and that may very well be the absolute best part of owning a bakery. We never miss a party or a reason to ramp up production to celebrate a holiday.

And the bakery itself feels like a party every day, with our festive pastel-colored and sparkly decorations that shine in the windows. It's not unusual for our customers to hold birthday parties, baby showers, and hen parties at our place, and we love it when they do—they make us feel a part of their celebrations too. Growing up, I always had my birthday parties at home, and it's such a nice compliment to know that our customers feel right at home in the bakery.

Holidays and special occasions are certainly not the time for a ho-hum dessert—they are when you pull out all the stops. So some of the desserts in this chapter may take a little extra time and planning, but we show you how to make them in clever ways so they won't be nearly as fussy as you might think. My secret ingredient is organization: make lists, and work your way down them bit by bit. If you have everything measured in advance, the baking part becomes fast and easy.

I always want to inspire you with some decorating tips that I use at the bakery and describe how to give all of your cakes handmade details that you'll be so proud to show off. Desserts like the Cakette Party Cake (page 156), Baby Cakes (page 152), Janie Q's Lemon Cake (page 172), Confetti Cupcakes (page 184), and the Festive Yule Log (page 192) will leave your friends and family impressed that you took the time to make these special creations from scratch.

If I'm not baking for the holidays, you'll find me crafting something for the celebration. The Cupcake Surprise Balls (page 262), which are a nod to the piñata parties of my youth, are filled with one of my favorite things—confetti! And you can adorn an honored party guest with the Baby-Cake Party Hat (page 87) and your cake with the Keepsake Cake Topper (page 197). Let the celebration begin!

BABY CAKES WITH VANILLA MERINGUE BUTTERCREAM

Makes 6 small cakes

The baby cake is one of the bakery's signature desserts; it's a sweet little party cake meant to be enjoyed by one special person for dessert (and perhaps a snack the next day).

We inherited our baby cake pans from our mentor, Jane Thompson, who made these cakes at Mondo Bakery in Atlanta, but we put our own spin on her idea. We make baby cakes in all flavors based on the season and the occasion and decorate them with roses, paper flags, and vintage toppers. We tinted the cakes shown here in pastel colors that are our signature shades. Imagine serving them at your party in your own favorite colors. Decorate the tops of the cakes with edible fresh flowers, buttercream flowers, candy necklaces, or paper flags: you can be as creative and fancy as you like.

3 cups cake flour (not self-rising)
4 teaspoons baking powder, preferably aluminum-free
½ teaspoon fine sea salt
1 cup whole milk
1 teaspoon pure vanilla extract

½ pound (2 sticks) unsalted butter, at room temperature
2 cups granulated sugar
4 large eggs, separated, at room temperature
A few drops liquid gel food coloring (the color is your pick; use several colors if you like)

1 recipe Vanilla Meringue Buttercream (recipe follows)

SPECIAL EQUIPMENT
Six 4-inch round cake pans

Position a rack in the middle of the oven and preheat the oven to 350°F. Butter six 4-inch cake pans, line the bottoms with parchment, and butter the parchment as well. Lightly dust the pans with flour, tapping the pans on the counter to shake out the excess.

Sift together the flour, baking powder, and salt. Set aside.

In a large measuring cup or a small bowl, whisk together the milk and vanilla. Set aside.

In the bowl of a stand mixer fitted with the paddle attachment (or in a large mixing bowl, using a handheld mixer), cream the butter and sugar on medium-high speed for 3 to 5 minutes, until light and fluffy. Turn the mixer speed down to low and add the egg yolks, beating until thoroughly combined and scraping down the sides of the bowl with a rubber spatula as necessary.

continued

I Knew You Were Coming

So I Baked A Cake

On low speed, add the flour mixture in thirds, alternating with the milk and vanilla and beginning and ending with flour, mixing until just combined. If using a stand mixer, transfer the batter to another large bowl. Wash and dry the mixer bowl and fit the mixer with the whisk attachment.

Put the egg whites in the mixer bowl (or a clean large mixing bowl) and beat with the whisk attachment or a handheld mixer (with clean beaters) until soft peaks form. Scoop up a little of the egg whites with a rubber spatula and gently stir them into the batter to lighten it and make it easier to fold in the rest of the egg whites. Gently fold in the remaining egg whites until thoroughly incorporated.

Tint the batter to the desired shade with a few drops of food coloring. You can make the batter all one color or use different colors for each cake. It's also fun to make an ombré effect, tinting the batter in one color in a range from light to dark.

Divide the batter among the prepared pans, using about 1 cup for each pan. Gently smooth the tops with a spatula. Firmly tap the pans on the counter to release any air bubbles.

Bake for 20 to 25 minutes, until a cake tester inserted in the center of a cake comes out clean. Let the cakes cool for 15 minutes, then remove from the pans, peel off the parchment, and cool completely on a wire rack.

To assemble the baby cakes: With a serrated knife, cut the little dome off the top of each cake so it is level. (Eat up—baker's treat!) Carefully slice each cake in half horizontally to make two layers, then flip the cakes over.

Remove the top part of each cake and set it to the side. Put a small ice cream scoop or a tablespoon of frosting in the middle of each bottom layer and spread it evenly with an offset spatula or a butter knife. Place the top layers back on top. Frost the tops and sides of the cakes (or leave the sides unfrosted and dust with confectioners' sugar).

The cakes are best served at room temperature, but they can be stored in the refrigerator for up to 3 days.

Tip: To use buttercream that has been chilled, remove it from the refrigerator and bring it to room temperature. Make sure that it is softened to room temperature before you use it; if the butter is too cold, the buttercream will break and be a hot mess! Transfer the buttercream to a stand mixer fitted with the paddle attachment (or use a handheld mixer) and beat on medium speed until soft and spreadable, 2 to 3 minutes.

Vanilla Meringue Buttercream | *Makes about 8 cups*

12 large egg whites
3 cups granulated sugar
½ teaspoon fine sea salt
2½ pounds unsalted butter, cut into
   ½-inch chunks, at room temperature
1 tablespoon pure vanilla extract

SPECIAL EQUIPMENT
Candy or instant-read thermometer

In the bowl of a stand mixer fitted with the whisk attachment (or in a heatproof metal bowl), whisk together the egg whites, sugar, and salt. Set the bowl over a saucepan of simmering water (do not let the bottom of the bowl touch the water) and cook, whisking constantly, until the sugar is dissolved. Rub the mixture between your fingers to make sure the sugar is dissolved; the mixture will be warm to the touch and register 140°F on a candy or instant-read thermometer.

Remove the bowl from the heat and attach it to the mixer stand (or use a handheld mixer). Beat on high speed until stiff peaks form and the meringue cools to room temperature, 3 to 5 minutes.

Once the mixture has cooled to room temperature, replace the whisk with the paddle attachment and begin adding the butter: Add the butter chunks a few at a time, waiting for it to be incorporated before adding more and scraping down the sides of the bowl as needed. Don't worry if the mixture begins to look curdled; if that happens, slow down and make sure you are completely incorporating the butter before adding more. When all of the butter has been added, add the vanilla and beat for another 1 to 2 minutes. The frosting should be smooth, thick, and glossy.

Use immediately. Or store it in an airtight container in the refrigerator for up to 1 week. To use buttercream that has been chilled, see the Tip.

CAKETTE PARTY CAKE WITH ITALIAN MERINGUE BUTTERCREAM

Serves 12 to 16

After our baby cakes became so popular, our customers requested a cake that could serve a bigger crowd. We created this cake, which is a little bit fancy—and looks like a party when you open the box. It is a delicate, light white cake, with a bit of buttermilk in the batter that gives it an extra-tender and moist crumb. The Italian meringue buttercream is made by beating together egg whites, a boiled sugar syrup, and lots of butter. It has a consistency similar to that of fluffy whipped cream and it is not as sweet as frostings made with confectioners' sugar. The flavor options with this frosting are endless; add a few drops of your favorite extract or liqueur. Folks have been begging me for this recipe for years, so here it is at last.

3 cups cake flour (not self-rising)

1½ teaspoons baking powder, preferably aluminum-free

¾ teaspoon baking soda

¾ teaspoon fine sea salt

¾ pound (3 sticks) unsalted butter, at room temperature

2⅓ cups granulated sugar

3 large egg whites

2 teaspoons pure vanilla extract

1½ cups buttermilk

1 recipe Italian Meringue Buttercream (recipe follows)

Position a rack in the middle of the oven and preheat the oven to 350°F. Butter a baking sheet, then line it with parchment, leaving an overhang on the two short ends of the pan. Butter the parchment as well, and dust with flour, tapping the pan on the counter to shake out the excess.

Sift together the flour, baking powder, baking soda, and salt. Set aside.

In the bowl of a stand mixer fitted with the paddle attachment (or in a large mixing bowl, using a handheld mixer), cream the butter and sugar on medium-high speed for 3 to 5 minutes, until light and fluffy. Scrape down the sides of the bowl. Turn the mixer speed down to low, add the egg whites and vanilla, and mix until completely incorporated.

With the mixer on low speed, add the flour mixture in thirds, alternating with the buttermilk and beginning and ending with flour, mixing until just combined.

Remove the bowl from the mixer and, using a rubber spatula, incorporate any ingredients hiding at the bottom of the bowl, making sure the batter is completely mixed. Pour the batter into the

prepared pan and gently smooth the top with a spatula. Tap the pan firmly on the counter to remove any air bubbles from the batter.

Bake for 20 to 25 minutes, until a cake tester inserted in the center of the cake comes out clean and the cake is lightly golden. Let the cake cool for 15 minutes, then carefully remove it using the parchment "handles" from the pan, to cool completely on a wire rack. Peel off the parchment.

To assemble the cake: Cut the cake in half and then in half again, making 4 pieces. Place the first piece upside down on a serving plate (you can keep the edges of the plate clean while you frost the cake by sliding strips of parchment underneath the cake). Using an offset spatula, spread the layer with a big dollop of the buttercream. Place a second layer upside down on the first layer and frost the top. Repeat with the third layer. Then put the final layer on top, upside down. Frost the top and sides of the cake with a thin layer of frosting—the crumb coat—and set in the refrigerator to chill for at least 30 minutes.

Remove the cake from the refrigerator and frost with the remaining frosting. The cake is best served at room temperature, but it can stored in the refrigerator for up to 3 days.

Tip: I like to decorate my cakes to give them a homemade look by creating texture in the frosting using a spatula or a butter knife, or making big swirls with an offset spatula or the back of a spoon. Don't worry about getting the frosting perfectly smooth. It's handmade! Then decorate the top of the cake with edible fresh flowers, buttercream flowers, or paper flags. There are no rules, so decorate as you like.

ITALIAN MERINGUE BUTTERCREAM | *Makes 10 cups*

2 cups granulated sugar
½ cup water
10 large egg whites, at room temperature
1¼ teaspoons cream of tartar
2 pounds unsalted butter, cut into ½-inch
    chunks, at room temperature

1 tablespoon pure vanilla extract

SPECIAL EQUIPMENT
Candy thermometer

In a small saucepan, combine 1½ cups of the sugar and the water and cook over medium heat, stirring occasionally, until the sugar has dissolved. Brush down the sides of the saucepan with a pastry brush dipped in warm water to remove any crystals, then do not stir again. Clip a candy thermometer to the side of the saucepan and cook until the syrup reaches 248°F (the "soft ball stage"), 8 to 10 minutes. Keep a constant eye on the thermometer; timing is very important here.

Meanwhile, combine the egg whites and cream of tartar in the bowl of a stand mixer fitted with the whisk attachment (or use a large mixing bowl and a handheld mixer) and beat until the whites are foamy and barely hold soft peaks. Gradually add the remaining ½ cup sugar and then whisk for another 1 to 2 minutes, until the meringue holds soft peaks. Turn the mixer off.

As soon as the sugar syrup reaches 248°F, carefully lift the pan from the heat (use an oven mitt) and, with the mixer running on low, carefully pour the hot syrup into the egg white mixture in a slow, steady stream, avoiding the spinning whisk. Be careful: the syrup is very hot, and you don't want it to splash. Once all the syrup is added, raise the speed to high and beat until the meringue has cooled to room temperature, 8 to 12 minutes. It will have expanded greatly and will look like marshmallow cream. (The mixture will deflate as soon as you start adding butter.)

Once the mixture has cooled to room temperature, begin adding the butter. Switch to the paddle attachment if using a stand mixer and, beating on medium speed, drop in the butter a few chunks at a time, waiting for it to be incorporated each time before adding more and scraping down the sides of the bowl as needed. Don't worry if the mixture begins to look curdled; if that happens, slow down and make sure that you are completely incorporating the butter before adding more. When all of the butter has been incorporated, add the vanilla, raise the speed to high, and whip for 1 to 2 minutes. The buttercream should be smooth, thick, and glossy.

Use the buttercream immediately. Or store it in an airtight container in the refrigerator for up to 1 week. To use buttercream that has been chilled, see the Tip on page 186.

VARIATIONS

You can add different flavors to customize the frosting. For each 1 cup buttercream, add 3 tablespoons Lemon Curd (see page 172) or Raspberry Jam (page 266); and 1 tablespoon of your favorite liqueur, such as Grand Marnier, amaretto, or Chambord, and replace the vanilla with 1 tablespoon almond, mint, or coconut extract .

CARAMEL CAKE WITH SALTED CARAMEL FROSTING

Caramel cake is a true Southern American classic. The base is a delicate butter cake that is covered in a caramel frosting; we make a salted caramel version. Ours has a bit of caramel in the cake batter too, which makes it even richer. The best part is that you can make this cake a day ahead of your party, because the flavors get even better with time.

Serves
12 to 16

2½ cups unbleached all-purpose flour
2½ teaspoons baking powder, preferably aluminum-free
1 teaspoon fine sea salt
1 cup Salted Caramel Sauce (page 280)

½ cup water
1⅓ cups granulated sugar
8 tablespoons (1 stick) unsalted butter, at room temperature
3 large eggs, at room temperature

Salted Caramel Frosting (recipe follows)
Flaky sea salt, such as Jacobsen or Maldon, or fleur de sel for sprinkling

Position a rack in the lower third of the oven and preheat the oven to 350°F. Butter two 9-by-2-inch round cake pans, line the bottoms with parchment, and butter the parchment as well. Lightly dust the pans with flour, tapping the pans on the counter to shake out the excess.

Sift together the flour, baking powder, and fine sea salt. Set aside.

In a small bowl, combine the caramel sauce and water and stir until completely smooth. Set aside.

In the bowl of a stand mixer fitted with the paddle attachment (or in a large mixing bowl, using a handheld mixer), cream the sugar and butter together on medium-high speed for 3 to 5 minutes, until light and fluffy. Add the eggs one at a time, beating well after each addition and scraping down the sides of the bowl with a rubber spatula as necessary.

With the mixer on low speed, add the flour mixture in thirds, alternating with the caramel mixture and beginning and ending with flour, mixing just until combined. Scrape down the sides of the bowl with a rubber spatula as necessary.

Divide the batter evenly between the prepared pans and smooth the tops with a spatula.

continued

Bake for 25 to 30 minutes, until a cake tester inserted in the center of a cake layer comes out clean. Let the cakes cool for 20 minutes, then remove from the pans, peel off the parchment, and cool completely on a wire rack.

To assemble the cake: Level the top of one of the cake layers with a serrated knife so it is flat, then place it cut side down on a serving plate (you can keep the edges of the plate clean while you frost the cake by sliding strips of parchment underneath the cake). Using an offset spatula or a butter knife, spread the layer with a big dollop of frosting. Place the other cake layer top side up on the first layer and frost the top and sides with the remaining frosting, making big swirls with the spatula or butter knife. Sprinkle a little flaky sea salt over the top of the cake.

The cake is best served at room temperature, but it can stored in the refrigerator for up to 3 days.

SALTED CARAMEL FROSTING | *Makes about 5 cups*

2 cups packed dark brown sugar
12 tablespoons (1½ sticks) unsalted butter, cut into tablespoon-sized pieces
½ teaspoon fine sea salt
½ cup heavy cream
1½ teaspoons pure vanilla extract
2½ cups confectioners' sugar, sifted

In a heavy saucepan, combine the brown sugar, 8 tablespoons (1 stick) of the butter, and the salt and cook over medium heat, stirring constantly, until the mixture comes to a gentle boil, 5 to 8 minutes. Whisk in the cream and continue to cook until it comes to a boil again. Take off the heat and add the vanilla.

Pour the mixture into the bowl of a stand mixer fitted with the paddle attachment (or use a large mixing bowl and a handheld mixer) and, with the mixer on low speed, gradually add the confectioners' sugar, beating until incorporated. Turn the mixer up to medium speed and beat until the frosting is a pale brown and cooled to warm, 3 to 5 minutes. Add the remaining 4 tablespoons butter a little at a time and continue to mix until light and fluffy.

Use the frosting immediately.

Tip: When decorating cakes, I always take the time to apply a thin layer of frosting, called a "crumb coat," first and then refrigerate the cake for at least 30 minutes (or as long as overnight). This simple step traps any loose crumbs in that first layer of frosting so that the final layer of frosting will be smooth. It also keeps the cake in place (so you don't have a tipsy-topsy cake!). Put a bit of your frosting in a separate bowl for the crumb coat to keep the larger batch of frosting crumb-free. Then check the cake after it has set for about 10 minutes to make sure that it hasn't shifted. You can adjust it if necessary before the frosting has completely set.

HOW TO MAKE A TIERED CELEBRATION CAKE

There is nothing like a handmade celebration cake baked from scratch. Whether it's for a birthday or a wedding, it is absolutely the best gift you can ever give. Back in the day, celebration cakes were baked by the best baker in the family (or a close family friend) and given as a gift to the bride and groom. Griff and I still carry on this tradition today, and our closest friends always appreciate the gesture. So much time, effort, and love go into making a tiered celebration cake. The secret? Plan well in advance so that you can stay ahead of the unexpected. Once all of the elements are made, you can have fun and leave only the decorating for the night before the party. *Makes one 6- or 7-layer 2-tier celebration cake; serves 25 to 30*

It's as easy as 1, 2, 3, 4.
DAYS ONE AND TWO: Bake the cake layers and make the simple syrup
DAY THREE: Make the buttercream and assemble the cake
DAY FOUR: Decorate the cake

WHAT YOU'LL NEED

2 recipes Cakette Party Cake batter (page 156)
4 cups Simple Syrup (page 171)
2 recipes Italian Meringue Buttercream (page 159)

Three 9-inch and three 6-inch round cake pans
Three 9-inch and three 6-inch cardboard cake rounds (see Resources, page 293)

Decorating turntable
One 10- to 12-inch cake stand plate
4 plastic drinking straws

Days 1 and 2: To bake the cakes: Position the racks in the middle and lower third of the oven and preheat the oven to 350°F. Butter three 6-inch round cake pans and three 9-inch round cake pans. Line the bottoms with parchment and butter that as well. Lightly dust the pans with flour, tapping the pans on the counter to shake out the excess.

Pour the batter into the pans, using about 2 cups batter for each 6-inch pan and about 3 cups for each 9-inch pan. Smooth the tops and tap the pans on the counter to remove any air bubbles. Bake until the cakes are lightly golden, and a cake tester inserted in the center of a cake comes out clean: the 6-inch cake layers need 20 to 25 minutes, and the 9-inch layers need 30 to 35 minutes. Let the cakes cool for 15 minutes, then remove from the pans, peel off the parchment, and cool completely on wire racks.

Double-wrap the cooled layers in plastic and label them with the date. The cakes can be kept at room temperature for up to 2 days or refrigerated for up to 3 days. You can also freeze them for up to a week; transfer them to the refrigerator the night before you are ready to assemble the cake.

To prepare the cake layers: Level the tops of all of the cake layers with a serrated knife. Put a dab of frosting on a 6-inch cardboard cake round (to anchor the cake) and put one of the small layers cut side down on the round, then put it on a decorating turntable. Brush the layer generously with simple syrup (about 2 tablespoons). Using an offset spatula or a butter knife, spread the layer with a big dollop of frosting. Place another 6-inch cake layer upside down on top and brush with syrup. Frost the top and sides with a thin layer of frosting (the crumb coat). Refrigerate for at least 1 hour, then repeat with the final layer. Repeat the same process with the 9-inch cake layers. Once the frosting is set, wrap the tiers in plastic wrap and refrigerate until ready to assemble the cake.

Day 3: To assemble the cake: Remove the 9-inch tier from the refrigerator. Using an offset spatula or a butter knife, apply another thicker layer of frosting over the top and sides. Then decorate the tier, making big or small swirls with the spatula or butter knife to create texture. Return to the refrigerator to chill and repeat with the 6-inch tier. Return to the refrigerator to chill.

Remove the 9-inch tier from the refrigerator and put it on the cake stand (or plate). Insert a plastic straw vertically through the center of the tier, mark the straw with kitchen shears at the point where it is level with the top of the cake, and remove the straw. Using the shears, cut the straw at the marked point. Using the straw as a guide, cut 3 more straws to this length. Press a 6-inch cardboard round gently down on the cake to make an outline of where the top tier should go. Insert the 4 straws at regular intervals just inside the circle outline to support the top tier (and keep it level), spacing them evenly. Position the 6-inch tier on top of the straws. Step back to admire your work. You did it!

Day 4: Finish decorating the cake as desired and top it off with vintage toppers, edible fresh flowers, or the Keepsake Cake Topper (page 197).

continued

CAKE-BUILDING STEP-BY-STEP

Apply a dab of frosting to the cardboard cake round.

Brush the cake layer with simple syrup to keep it moist.

Spread a thin coat of frosting over the cake layer.

Add another cake layer and frost the top again.

Add the top cake layer so the bottom side is on the bottom, creating a flat surface.

Apply a thin layer of frosting to the top and sides of the cake.

Insert cut straws to create support for the second tier of cake.

Place the second tier on top of the first tier.

Finish the cake by applying the remaining frosting.

Add your favorite decorations to make the cake pretty.

You did it!

CHOCOLATE CREAM CAKE WITH DARK CHOCOLATE GANACHE

The light, delicate texture of this cake paired with a creamy whipped vanilla buttercream filling and dark chocolate ganache coating is like a dream come true (or at least my dream!). I like to put coffee in my chocolate cake batter because it really makes the flavor sing.

Serves 12 to 16

2⅓ cups cake flour (not self-rising)
1 cup Dutch-processed cocoa powder
1½ teaspoons baking soda
1 teaspoon fine sea salt
¼ teaspoon baking powder, preferably aluminum-free
1 cup hot strong coffee
1 cup buttermilk

½ pound (2 sticks) unsalted butter, at room temperature
2½ cups granulated sugar
4 large eggs, at room temperature
1 large egg yolk, at room temperature
2 teaspoons pure vanilla extract

¼ pound semisweet chocolate, melted and slightly cooled

½ cup Simple Syrup (see the Sweet Note)
1 recipe Whipped Buttercream Frosting (page 181)
1 recipe Dark Chocolate Ganache (recipe follows)

Position a rack in the middle of the oven and preheat the oven to 350°F. Butter three 9-by-2-inch round cake pans, then line the bottoms with parchment and butter that as well. Lightly dust the pans with flour, tapping the pans on the counter to shake out the excess.

Sift together the flour, cocoa, baking soda, salt, and baking powder. Set aside.

In a small bowl, whisk together the hot coffee and buttermilk. Set aside.

In the bowl of a stand mixer fitted with the paddle attachment (or in a large mixing bowl, using a handheld mixer), cream the butter and sugar on medium-high speed for 3 to 5 minutes, until light and fluffy. Turn the mixer speed down to low and add the eggs and yolk one at a time, mixing well after each addition. Add the vanilla and mix until combined. Then mix on high speed until the batter is doubled in volume and very light and fluffy, about 3 minutes. Scrape down the sides of the bowl with a rubber spatula and mix for another minute.

continued

On low speed, add the flour mixture in thirds, alternating with the coffee and buttermilk mixture and beginning and ending with flour, mixing until just combined. Beat in the melted chocolate.

Remove the bowl from the mixer and, using a rubber spatula, incorporate any ingredients hiding at the bottom of the bowl, making sure the batter is completely mixed. Divide the batter evenly among the prepared pans and smooth the tops.

Bake for 25 to 30 minutes, until a cake tester inserted in the center of a cake comes out clean. Let the cakes cool for 20 minutes, then remove from the pans, peel off the parchment, and cool completely on a wire rack.

To assemble the cake: Using a serrated knife, level the top of 2 of the cake layers. Place one layer cut side down on a serving plate (you can keep the edges of the plate clean while you frost the cake by sliding strips of parchment underneath the cake). Generously brush some simple syrup on top of the cake layer. Using an offset spatula or a butter knife, spread the layer with a big dollop of frosting. Place the second cake layer cut side down on top and repeat. Place the final cake layer right side up on top and frost the top with another big dollop of frosting. Place the cake in the refrigerator for at least 1 hour, or overnight, to set the frosting.

Using an offset spatula or a butter knife, frost the top and sides of the cake with the ganache. Finish decorating by making big swirls with the spatula or butter knife. The cake is ready to celebrate.

The cake can be stored, wrapped in plastic wrap, in the refrigerator for up to 3 days.

DARK CHOCOLATE GANACHE | *Makes about 3 cups*

1 cup heavy cream
8 tablespoons (1 stick) unsalted butter, cut into 1-inch pieces
⅓ cup granulated sugar
¼ teaspoon fine sea salt
1 pound semisweet chocolate, finely chopped
¼ cup hot coffee
1 teaspoon pure vanilla extract

Combine the cream, butter, sugar, and salt in a heatproof bowl, set it over a saucepan of simmering water (do not let the bottom of the bowl touch the water), and stir occasionally until the butter is melted. Add the chocolate and stir until it is completely melted and the mixture is smooth.

Take off the heat and stir in the coffee and vanilla until smooth, then stir occasionally as the ganache cools and thickens. Making the perfect ganache cannot be rushed: resist the urge to refrigerate it or whisk it to cool it faster. Once it is thickened and glistening, you are ready to decorate your cake.

HOW TO MAKE SIMPLE SYRUP

Brushing cake layers with a flavored simple syrup works to keep the cake layers moist and adds another element of flavor as well.

If you want to make a citrus syrup, substitute 1 cup fresh orange, lemon, or lime juice for the water. You can also mix flavors, such as vanilla, almond, and coconut extract. Or infuse the plain syrup with fresh herbs, like lavender or chamomile, or add 1 to 2 teaspoons of your favorite liqueur, such as Grand Marnier, St-Germain, or amaretto.

To use the syrup, poke several holes in each cake layer using a toothpick and brush the syrup generously on the layers. Allow the syrup to soak in for a few minutes before frosting and assembling the cake. *Makes about 2 cups*

1 cup water
1 cup granulated sugar (or 1 cup packed light brown sugar)
**1 teaspoon pure vanilla extract (or other extract of your choice, such as lemon
   or almond)**

Combine the water and sugar in a medium saucepan and heat over medium heat, stirring, until the sugar completely dissolves. Add the extract, bring the syrup to a boil, and boil for 3 to 5 minutes, until it starts to thicken.

Let cool before using; or label and refrigerate in an airtight container or a heat-sterilized Mason jar for up to 1 month.

JANIE Q'S LEMON CAKE WITH LEMON MERINGUE BUTTERCREAM

My mom was the queen of lemon meringue pie. (Her name was really Janie Queen!) I created this cake in her honor; I wanted to convey her happy personality in cake form. It's a light and delicate cake filled with a fresh bright lemon curd and covered in a luscious lemon meringue buttercream. You will taste a bit of sunshine in every bite.

Serves 12 to 16

2½ cups cake flour (not self-rising)
2½ teaspoons baking powder, preferably aluminum-free
1 teaspoon fine sea salt
½ cup whole milk
1 teaspoon pure vanilla extract
½ pound (2 sticks) unsalted butter, at room temperature

1½ cups granulated sugar
2 tablespoons grated lemon zest
2 tablespoons fresh lemon juice
4 large eggs, at room temperature

FOR THE LEMON CURD
7 large egg yolks
1 cup granulated sugar
½ cup fresh lemon juice

4 tablespoons cold unsalted butter, cubed
1 tablespoon grated lemon zest

½ cup vanilla Simple Syrup (see page 171)
1 recipe Lemon Meringue Buttercream (recipe follows)
Lemon slices for decoration (optional)

Position a rack in the middle of the oven and preheat the oven to 350°F. Butter two 9-by-2-inch round cake pans, then line the bottoms with parchment and butter that as well. Lightly dust the pans with flour, tapping the pans on the counter to shake out the excess.

Sift together the flour, baking powder, and salt. Set aside.

In a measuring cup or a small bowl, whisk together the milk and vanilla. Set aside.

In the bowl of a stand mixer fitted with the paddle attachment (or in a large mixing bowl, using a handheld mixer), cream the butter and sugar with the lemon zest for 3 to 5 minutes, until light and fluffy. Beat in the lemon juice. Turn the mixer speed down to low and add the eggs one at a time, beating well after each addition and scraping down the sides of the bowl with a rubber spatula as necessary.

continued

On low speed, add the flour mixture in thirds, alternating with the milk and vanilla and beginning and ending with flour, mixing until just combined. Remove the bowl from the mixer and, using a rubber spatula, incorporate any ingredients hiding at the bottom of the bowl, making sure the batter is completely mixed.

Divide the batter evenly between the prepared pans and gently smooth the tops with a spatula. Tap the pans firmly on the counter to remove any air bubbles from the batter.

Bake for 25 to 35 minutes, until a cake tester inserted in the center of a cake comes out clean. Let the cakes cool for 15 minutes, then remove from the pans, peel off the parchment, and cool completely on a wire rack.

To make the lemon curd: Whisk the egg yolks, sugar, and lemon juice together in a heatproof bowl. Set the bowl over a medium saucepan of simmering water (do not let the bottom of the bowl touch the water) and cook, whisking frequently, until the mixture is thick and glossy, 8 to 10 minutes.

Remove the curd from the heat and strain through a fine-mesh sieve into a bowl to make sure that there are no pesky bits of eggs remaining. Let the curd cool for about 10 minutes.

Whisk the butter into the curd. Fold in the lemon zest. Place a piece of plastic wrap directly on the surface of the curd so that a skin doesn't form, poke a few holes in the plastic to create steam vents, and let cool to room temperature.

Store the curd in an airtight container in the refrigerator for up to 1 week. You can also freeze it for up to 3 months.

To assemble the cake: Using a serrated knife, level the top of one of the cake layers. Place the layer cut side up on a serving plate (you can keep the edges of the plate clean while you frost the cake by sliding strips of parchment underneath the cake). Generously brush simple syrup on top of the cake layer.

Fit a pastry bag with a large plain tip (or use a large ziplock bag, with a bottom corner snipped off) and fill the bag halfway with the buttercream. Chill the remaining buttercream. Pipe a circle on the border of the cake to create a dam. Using an offset spatula or a butter knife, spread a big dollop of lemon curd in the middle of the frosting dam. Place the second cake layer right side up on top and frost the top and sides with a thin layer of frosting (the crumb coat). Place the cake in the refrigerator for at least 1 hour, or overnight, to set the frosting.

Using an offset spatula or a butter knife, frost the top and sides of the cake with the remaining buttercream. Finish by making big swirls with the spatula or butter knife. Decorate with lemon slices, if desired.

The cake can be stored, wrapped in plastic wrap, in the refrigerator for up to 3 days. Bring to room temperature before serving.

Lemon Meringue Buttercream | *Makes about 4 cups*

6 large egg whites
1½ cups granulated sugar
¼ teaspoon fine sea salt
1¼ pounds (5 sticks) butter, cut into ½-inch chunks, at room temperature
1½ tablespoons grated lemon zest
2 tablespoons fresh lemon juice

OPTIONAL SPECIAL EQUIPMENT
Candy or instant-read thermometer

In the bowl of a stand mixer (or in a large heatproof bowl), whisk together the egg whites, sugar, and salt. Set the bowl over a saucepan of simmering water (do not let the bottom of the bowl touch the water) and cook, whisking constantly, until the sugar is dissolved. Rub the mixture between your fingers to make sure the sugar is dissolved; the mixture will be warm to the touch and register 140°F on a candy or instant-read thermometer.

Remove the bowl from the heat, attach it to the mixer stand, and fit with the whisk attachment (or use a handheld mixer). Beat on high speed until stiff peaks form and the meringue cools to room temperature, 3 to 5 minutes.

Once the mixture has cooled to room temperature, replace the whisk with the paddle attachment and begin adding the butter. Add the butter chunks a few at a time, waiting for it to be incorporated before adding more and scraping down the sides of the bowl as needed. Don't worry if the mixture begins to look curdled; if that happens, slow down and make sure you are completely incorporating the butter before adding more. When all of the butter has been added, add the lemon zest and lemon juice and beat for another 1 to 2 minutes. The frosting should be smooth, thick, and glossy

Use the buttercream immediately. Or store it in an airtight container in the refrigerator for up to 1 week. To use buttercream that has been chilled, see the Tip on page 186.

ALABAMA LANE CAKE

*Serves
12 to 16*

Lane Cake is mentioned several times in one of my all-time favorite novels, *To Kill a Mockingbird*; it even stirs up a rivalry between two of the neighborhood home bakers. This old-timey cake, which is also known as Prize Cake, was created by Emma Rylander Lane of Alabama, who won first prize with it at the county fair in Columbus, Georgia, at the turn of the twentieth century. It's a moist white cake filled and frosted with a whiskey-laced custard, coconut, dried fruit, and pecans. The flavors are even better the next day (and the day after that). Lane Cake has been a tradition in my family for generations. We always serve it for celebrations and especially at Christmastime, and it has memories built into every slice.

3½ cups cake flour (not self-rising)
1 tablespoon baking powder, preferably aluminum-free
¼ teaspoon fine sea salt
1 cup whole milk
1 teaspoon pure vanilla extract

½ pound (2 sticks) unsalted butter, at room temperature
2 cups granulated sugar
8 large egg whites

FOR THE FROSTING
1½ cups pecans
12 tablespoons (1½ sticks) unsalted butter

1½ cups granulated sugar
12 large egg yolks
1½ cups sweetened flaked coconut
1½ cups golden raisins, finely chopped
½ cup bourbon or brandy

OPTIONAL SPECIAL EQUIPMENT
Instant-read thermometer

Position a rack in the middle of the oven and preheat the oven to 350°F. Butter three 9-by-2-inch round cake pans, line the bottoms with parchment, and butter that as well. Lightly dust the pans with flour, tapping the pans on the counter to shake out the excess.

Sift together the flour, baking powder, and salt. Set aside.

In a measuring cup or a small bowl, combine the milk and vanilla. Set aside.

In the bowl of a stand mixer fitted with the paddle attachment (or in a large mixing bowl, using a handheld mixer), cream the butter and sugar on medium-high speed for 3 to 5 minutes, until light and fluffy. Turn the mixer speed down to low and add the flour mixture in thirds, alternating with the milk and beginning and ending with flour, mixing just until combined; scrape down the sides of the bowl with a rubber spatula as necessary. If using a stand mixer, transfer to another large bowl.

continued

In the very clean mixer bowl (or in another large bowl), using the clean whisk (or clean beaters), beat the egg whites until they hold soft peaks. Fold one-quarter of the egg whites into the cake batter to lighten it, then gently fold in the remaining egg whites until incorporated.

Divide the batter evenly between the prepared pans and smooth the tops with a spatula. Bake for 25 to 30 minutes, until a cake tester inserted in the center of a cake comes out clean. Let the cake cool for 15 minutes, then remove from the pans, peel off the parchment, and cool completely on a wire rack.

To make the frosting: Preheat the oven to 350°F.

Spread the pecans on a baking sheet and toast in the oven for 6 to 8 minutes. Set aside to cool, then finely chop.

In a medium saucepan, melt the butter. Remove from the heat and let cool to tepid, then whisk in the sugar and egg yolks until smooth.

Set the pan over medium heat and cook, stirring constantly with a wooden spoon, until the filling has thickened enough to coat the back of the spoon; it should read 180°F on an instant-read thermometer. Be careful not to let the mixture come to a boil.

Remove from the heat and add the toasted pecans, coconut, golden raisins, and bourbon, stirring well. Transfer the frosting to a heatproof bowl to cool; it will continue to thicken as it cools. It will be ooey and gooey, and that is exactly what you want.

To assemble the cake: Level the top of 2 of the cake layers with a serrated knife. Place one layer cut side down on a serving plate (you can keep the edges of the plate clean while you frost the cake by sliding strips of parchment underneath the cake). Using an offset spatula or a butter knife, spread the layer with one-third of the frosting. Place the second cake layer cut side down and spread with another third of the frosting. Place the final layer right side up on top and frost the top with the remaining frosting.

The cake can be stored at room temperature for up to 2 days or refrigerated for 4 days. Serve at room temperature.

COCONUT CUPCAKES WITH WHIPPED BUTTERCREAM FROSTING

These coconut cupcakes are one of Griff's favorite treats. He loves the tender sweetness of coconut on top of the lightest buttercream frosting this side of the Mississippi. The hint of cardamom in the batter adds a delicate floral flavor.

Makes 24 cupcakes

3 cups unbleached all-purpose flour
1 teaspoon baking powder, preferably aluminum-free
½ teaspoon baking soda
1½ teaspoons fine sea salt
½ teaspoon ground cardamom

¾ pound (3 sticks) unsalted butter, at room temperature
2 cups granulated sugar
5 large eggs, at room temperature
1 teaspoon pure vanilla extract
1 cup buttermilk

¾ cup sweetened flaked coconut

1 recipe Whipped Buttercream Frosting (recipe follows)
2 cups sweetened flaked coconut

Position a rack in the middle of the oven and preheat the oven to 350°F. Line 24 cupcake cups with paper liners.

Sift together the flour, baking powder, baking soda, salt, and cardamom. Set aside.

In the bowl of a stand mixer fitted with the paddle attachment (or in a large mixing bowl, using a handheld mixer), cream the butter and sugar on medium-high speed for 3 to 5 minutes, until light and fluffy. Turn the mixer speed down to low and add the eggs one at a time, beating well after each addition, and scraping down the sides of the bowl with a rubber spatula as necessary. Add the vanilla and mix until combined.

On low speed, add the flour mixture in thirds, alternating with the buttermilk and beginning and ending with flour, mixing until just incorporated.

Remove the bowl from the mixer and, using a rubber spatula, incorporate any ingredients hiding at the bottom of the bowl, making sure the batter is completely mixed. Fold in the coconut.

continued

With a large ice cream scoop or spoon, scoop the batter into the prepared cupcake cups, filling them about two-thirds full. Bake for 20 to 25 minutes, until a cake tester inserted in the center of a cupcake comes out clean. Let cool for 20 minutes in the pans, then remove from the pans and cool completely on a wire rack.

To frost the cupcakes: Use a spatula or a butter knife to spread the tops of the cupcakes generously with the buttercream. Put the coconut in a medium bowl and dunk the tops in coconut to cover.

The cupcakes can be stored in an airtight container at room temperature for up to 2 days.

WHIPPED BUTTERCREAM FROSTING | *Makes 3½ cups*

¼ cup unbleached all-purpose flour
1 cup whole milk
½ pound (2 sticks) unsalted butter, at room temperature
1 teaspoon pure vanilla extract
1 cup granulated sugar

Combine the flour and ¼ cup of the milk in a small heavy saucepan and whisk until blended. Set the pan over medium heat and gradually add the remaining ¾ cup milk, whisking constantly, then cook, whisking, until the mixture comes to a low boil. Reduce the heat to low and whisk until the mixture begins to thicken and starts to "burp," 2 to 3 minutes.

Transfer the mixture to a small heatproof bowl and stir occasionally as it cools to keep it lump-free. If you do get a few lumps, don't worry—you can whisk the mixture to dissolve the lumps, or pass it through a fine-mesh sieve. (You can put the mixture in the refrigerator for 10 minutes to speed up the cooling process.)

In the bowl of a stand mixer fitted with the whisk attachment (or in a large bowl, using a handheld mixer), whip the butter and vanilla on medium speed until soft and creamy, 2 to 3 minutes. Gradually add the sugar and then beat on high speed until the mixture is light and fluffy, 5 to 7 minutes.

Reduce the speed to low and gradually add the milk mixture, then increase the speed to medium-high and whip until the frosting is light and fluffy, scraping down the sides of the bowl with a rubber spatula as necessary.

Use the frosting immediately. Or store in an airtight container in the refrigerator for up to 2 days. To use buttercream that has been chilled, see the Tip on page 186.

GINGERBREAD CUPCAKES WITH LEMON–CREAM CHEESE FROSTING

Makes 24 cupcakes

The snap of spice and the warmth of gingerbread always makes it the treat of choice for me on a cool fall day. When topped with a lemony frosting, these gingerbread cupcakes get a fresh burst of flavor. During the holidays, I like to deck these out with decorated mini sugar cookies made from scraps of dough for festive treats. For an added bonus, when you bake these, the aroma of ginger, cinnamon, and allspice will fill your kitchen with holiday cheer.

3 cups unbleached all-purpose flour
1½ teaspoons ground ginger
1 teaspoon baking soda
1 teaspoon ground cinnamon
½ teaspoon fine sea salt

½ teaspoon ground allspice
½ pound (2 sticks) unsalted butter, at room temperature
1 cup packed light brown sugar
4 large eggs, at room temperature
1 cup buttermilk

2 tablespoons light unsulfured molasses
2 teaspoons pure vanilla extract

1 recipe Lemon–Cream Cheese Frosting (recipe follows)

Position a rack in the middle of the oven and preheat the oven to 350°F. Line 24 cupcake cups with paper liners.

Sift together the flour, ginger, baking soda, cinnamon, salt, and allspice. Set aside.

In the bowl of a stand mixer fitted with the paddle attachment (or in a large mixing bowl, using a handheld mixer), cream the butter and brown sugar on medium-high speed for 3 to 5 minutes, until light and fluffy. Turn the mixer speed down to low and add the eggs one at a time, beating well after each addition and scraping down the sides of the bowl with a rubber spatula as necessary.

With the mixer on low speed, add the flour mixture in three additions, alternating with the buttermilk and beginning and ending with flour, mixing just until incorporated. Add the molasses and vanilla.

Remove the bowl from the mixer and, using a rubber spatula, incorporate any ingredients hiding at the bottom of the bowl, making sure the batter is completely mixed. With a large ice cream scoop or spoon, scoop the batter into the prepared cupcake cups, filling each one about two-thirds full.

Bake for 20 to 25 minutes, until a cake tester inserted in the center of a cupcake comes out clean. Let cool for 15 minutes in the pans, then remove from the pans and cool completely on a wire rack.

To frost the cupcakes: Use a spatula or a butter knife to spread the tops of the cupcakes generously with the cream cheese frosting.

The cupcakes can be refrigerated for up to 2 days. Bring to room temperature before serving.

LEMON–CREAM CHEESE FROSTING | *Makes about 5 cups*

Two 8-ounce packages cream cheese, at room temperature
8 tablespoons (1 stick) unsalted butter, at room temperature
2 teaspoons grated lemon zest
1 tablespoon fresh lemon juice
5 to 6 cups confectioners' sugar

In the bowl of a stand mixer fitted with the paddle attachment (or in a large bowl, using a handheld mixer), beat the cream cheese, butter, lemon zest, and lemon juice on medium speed until smooth and creamy, 2 to 3 minutes. Gradually add 5 cups of the confectioners' sugar, then add up to 1 cup more sugar if the frosting seems thin, and beat on high speed until light and fluffy, 5 to 7 minutes.

The frosting can be used immediately or covered and refrigerated for up to 5 days.

CONFETTI CUPCAKES WITH ALL-AMERICAN BUTTERCREAM FROSTING

These cupcakes are great for celebrating a birthday—and they're not just for kids. Filled with sprinkles, they are light and fluffy and topped with a classic buttercream frosting made with confectioners' sugar and butter. If you have a sweet craving, these cupcakes are sure to give you a fix.

Makes 24 cupcakes

1 cup whole milk

5 large egg whites

2 teaspoons pure vanilla extract

3 cups cake flour (not self-rising)

1½ cups granulated sugar

4 teaspoons baking powder, preferably non-aluminum

¼ teaspoon fine sea salt

12 tablespoons (1½ sticks) unsalted butter, cut into 1-inch chunks, at room temperature

⅓ cup multicolored sprinkles or jimmies

1 recipe All-American Buttercream Frosting (recipe follows)

Position a rack in the middle of the oven and preheat the oven to 350°F. Line 24 cupcake cups with paper liners.

In a large measuring cup or a small bowl, whisk together ¼ cup of the milk, the egg whites, and vanilla. Set aside.

In the bowl of a stand mixer fitted with the paddle attachment (or in a large mixing bowl, using a handheld mixer), mix the flour, sugar, baking powder, and salt on low speed until thoroughly combined. With the mixer on low speed, add the butter a few pieces at a time, mixing until the mixture resembles coarse sand. Gradually add the remaining ¾ cup milk and beat for 1 to 2 minutes. Scrape down the sides of the bowl with a rubber spatula.

With the mixer on medium speed, gradually add the egg mixture in thirds, mixing well after each addition and scraping down the bowl as necessary. Gently fold in the sprinkles.

With a large ice cream scoop or spoon, scoop the batter into the prepared cupcake cups, filling them about two-thirds full.

continued

Bake for 20 to 25 minutes, until a cake tester inserted in the center of a cupcake comes out clean. Let cool for 15 minutes, then remove from the pans and cool completely on a wire rack.

To frost the cupcakes: Use a spatula or a butter knife to spread the tops of the cupcakes with big swirls of the buttercream frosting.

The cupcakes can be stored in an airtight container at room temperature for up to 2 days.

ALL-AMERICAN BUTTERCREAM FROSTING | *Makes about 6 cups*

½ pound (2 sticks) unsalted butter, at room temperature
6 to 7 cups confectioners' sugar
½ cup whole milk
2 teaspoons pure vanilla extract
A few drops of liquid gel food coloring (optional)

In the bowl of a stand mixer fitted with the paddle attachment (or in a large mixing bowl, using a handheld mixer), cream the butter on medium speed for 2 to 3 minutes, until light and fluffy. Add 4 cups of the confectioners' sugar, ¼ cup of the milk, and the vanilla and mix on low speed for 2 to 3 minutes, until smooth and creamy. Add the remaining ¼ cup milk and mix until incorporated, 1 to 2 minutes. Gradually add 2 cups more sugar, then add up to 1 cup more sugar if the frosting seems thin, and beat on low speed for 3 to 5 minutes, until the frosting is light and fluffy.

If desired, tint the frosting: Add a drop or two of food coloring to the frosting, mixing well, then add more coloring as necessary until you reach the desired shade. Or, if you want multiple colors, scoop the frosting into several bowls, then add food coloring.

The frosting can be used immediately or stored in an airtight container (or containers) at room temperature for up to 2 days or refrigerated for up to 1 week.

Tip: To use buttercream that has been chilled, remove from the refrigerator and bring to room temperature; make sure that it is softened to room temperature before you use it. Then transfer the buttercream to the bowl of a stand mixer fitted with the paddle attachment (or to a bowl, and use a handheld mixer) and beat on medium-high until light and fluffy, 2 to 3 minutes.

BUTTERMILK BROWN SUGAR CHEESECAKE WITH SORGHUM-CARAMEL PECANS

I have learned through trial and error that the secret to making a perfect cheesecake is to bake it low and slow. Make it a day in advance and chill it overnight so you can serve it good and cold. This one, made with buttermilk, brown sugar, and cardamom, is accented by the fruity notes of sorghum, and is topped with Sorghum-Caramel Pecans and then with Salted Caramel Sauce.

*Serves
12 to 16*

FOR THE CRUST

1½ cups gingersnap crumbs
   (about 30 gingersnaps)
2 tablespoons granulated
   sugar
¼ teaspoon fine sea salt
6 tablespoons unsalted
   butter, melted

FOR THE FILLING

Five 8-ounce packages
   (2½ pounds) cream
   cheese, at room
   temperature
1½ cups packed light
   brown sugar
6 large eggs, at room
   temperature
3 large egg yolks, at room
   temperature
⅓ cup buttermilk

¼ teaspoon ground
   cardamom
1 tablespoon sorghum or
   honey
1 teaspoon pure vanilla
   extract

1 recipe Sorghum-Caramel
   Pecans (recipe follows)
1 cup Salted Caramel Sauce
   (page 280)

Position a rack in the lower third of the oven and preheat the oven to 350°F. Butter a 10-inch springform pan and wrap the bottom and sides in heavy-duty aluminum foil.

To make the crust: In a medium bowl, mix together the gingersnap crumbs, sugar, and salt. Drizzle in the butter and mix with a fork until the crumbs are evenly moistened. Press the mixture evenly into the bottom of the prepared pan—use a piece of parchment to press on the crust to make sure it is completely level. Pop into the freezer for about 15 minutes to set the crust.

Bake the crust for 8 to 10 minutes, until lightly golden. Let cool completely before filling. Increase the oven temperature to 400°F.

continued

To make the filling: In the bowl of a stand mixer fitted with the paddle attachment (or in a large mixing bowl, using a handheld mixer), beat the cream cheese on medium-high speed for about 5 minutes, until light and fluffy. Reduce the speed to low, gradually add the sugar, and beat for 3 to 5 minutes, until light and fluffy. Add the eggs and egg yolks 3 at a time, beating well after each addition. Scrape down the paddle and the sides of the bowl.

Add the buttermilk, cardamom, sorghum, and vanilla and mix for 3 to 5 minutes, until the filling is the consistency of sour cream.

Pour the filling into the cooled crust, then place the springform pan in a large deep baking pan. Add enough hot water to the baking pan to come halfway up the sides of the springform pan.

Bake for 10 minutes, then turn the oven temperature down to 225°F and bake the cheesecake for another 1 hour and 15 minutes, or until it is firm on the edges and the center no longer looks wet but still wobbles slightly. It will continue to set as it cools. Turn the oven off and leave the cheesecake in the oven, with the door partially open, for 30 minutes.

Take the cheesecake out of the water bath and allow it to cool to room temperature, 3 to 4 hours. Once it is cooled, carefully wrap the cheesecake, still in the pan, in aluminum foil and refrigerate overnight, until thoroughly chilled.

When ready to serve, run a hot knife around the edges of the pan to loosen the cheesecake, then remove the springform sides. Carefully transfer the cake to a serving plate. Top the cake with the caramel pecans and caramel sauce.

The cheesecake, which is best served chilled, can be stored in an airtight container in the refrigerator for up to 5 days.

SORGHUM-CARAMEL PECANS | *Makes 2 cups*

4 tablespoons unsalted butter, melted
½ teaspoon ground cinnamon
½ teaspoon freshly grated nutmeg
½ teaspoon ground mace
½ teaspoon ground cardamom
¼ cup sorghum
1 teaspoon fine sea salt
2 cups pecans

Position a rack in the middle of the oven and preheat the oven to 325°F. Line a baking sheet with parchment.

continued

In a medium bowl, combine the butter, cinnamon, nutmeg, mace, cardamom, sorghum, and salt, mixing well. Add the pecans, tossing to coat evenly.

Spread the nuts out in a single layer in the prepared baking sheet. Bake for 6 to 8 minutes, until they start to brown. Let cool completely.

Stored in an airtight container, the nuts will keep for up to 1 week.

SORGHUM IS LIQUID GOLD

Sorghum is one of my favorite ingredients. Its flavor is very complex: rich, sweet, fruity, caramely, and a little earthy, all at the same time. It is like liquid gold in our kitchen because it gives such character to everything it touches.

Sorghum syrup is a Southern ingredient that dates back to the mid-1800s. Traditionally sorghum production was a family-centered business, and even today it is still made by a few families who honor the history and Old World methods of milling sorghum by horse or mule, crushing the stalks, and then cooking the syrup in large vats over an open fire.

Although it is often referred to as sorghum molasses because it is thick, golden, and rich, sorghum is not molasses at all. It is made from the stalks of sweet sorghum cane, while molasses is a by-product of refined sugar.

Sorghum is often used in biscuits, pies, and cakes, but you can also add a little to soups, sauces, and vinaigrettes. You will find sorghum in many recipes throughout this book, and I buy cases of the stuff for the bakery now—but that doesn't stop me from buying a bottle from a small producer whenever I see it when I am traveling.

FESTIVE YULE LOG

Serves 12 to 16

Our Southern spin on the traditional French bûche de Noël is made with chiffon cake, espresso buttercream, and a rich chocolate buttercream, and it's decorated with sugared cranberries and rosemary sprigs and pistachio "moss"; you can use some or all of these and any other festive additions you like. Let me warn you, this recipe is a labor of love, but it is so fun to make, and you can spread out the steps over a couple of days. It's a showstopping centerpiece for your Christmas table.

¼ cup vegetable oil

4 large eggs, separated, at room temperature

⅓ cup plus 1 tablespoon water

1½ teaspoons pure vanilla extract

1 cup plus 2 tablespoons unbleached all-purpose flour

1 teaspoon baking powder, preferably aluminum-free

¾ cup granulated sugar

½ teaspoon fine sea salt

2 large egg whites

¼ teaspoon cream of tartar or fresh lemon juice

FOR THE COFFEE SYRUP

¼ cup strong coffee, hot

¼ cup granulated sugar

1 recipe Whipped Espresso Buttercream (recipe follows)

1 recipe Classic Chocolate Buttercream (page 70)

Sugared Rosemary and Cranberries, Pistachio Moss, and/or other decorations; see the Sweet Note (page 196)

SPECIAL EQUIPMENT

A plastic drinking straw

Position a rack in the lower third of the oven and preheat the oven to 325°F. Line a baking sheet with parchment.

In a small bowl, whisk together the oil, egg yolks, water, and vanilla. Set aside.

Sift together the flour and baking powder into a large bowl. Add ½ cup plus 1 tablespoon of the sugar and the salt and whisk to combine. Make a well in the center of the flour mixture, add the egg yolk mixture, and whisk briskly until very smooth, about 1 minute.

In the bowl of a stand mixer fitted with the whisk attachment (or in a large bowl, using a handheld mixer), beat all the egg whites on medium speed until frothy. Add the cream of tartar and beat on medium-high speed until the whites hold soft peaks. Slowly add the remaining 3 tablespoons sugar and beat until the whites hold firm, shiny peaks.

continued

Using a rubber spatula, scoop about one-third of the whites onto the yolk mixture and fold in gently to lighten the batter. Gently but thoroughly fold in the remaining whites just until combined.

Pour the batter into the prepared pan, smoothing the top with an offset spatula. Bake for 20 to 25 minutes, until the cake is just set to the touch. Let cool completely on a rack. The cake can be stored in the refrigerator, well wrapped, for up to 3 days.

To make the coffee syrup: In a small bowl, mix together the coffee and sugar, stirring until the sugar dissolves. Set aside.

To assemble the Yule Log: Invert the cake onto a piece of parchment and peel off the top sheet of parchment. Using a pastry brush, moisten the cake with the coffee syrup. With an offset spatula, spread the espresso buttercream evenly over the cake, leaving a 1-inch border on the long sides. Starting from a long side, roll up the cake, using the parchment to help you lift and roll it evenly and tightly. The cake may crack as you roll, but don't worry, just continue to roll. Refrigerate the rolled cake until the buttercream is firm, about 2 hours.

To frost and decorate the log: Using a sharp knife, trim off the ends of the log, about ½ inch on each end. Cut a 6-inch piece from one end of the log and cut it diagonally in half.

Place the log seam side down on a serving platter (you can keep the edges of the platter clean while you frost the cake by sliding strips of parchment under the cake). Use a small offset spatula to place 2 dollops of the chocolate buttercream on the top to anchor the branches. Place one "branch" slanted side up on top of the log. Cut a plastic straw in half and insert one piece into the bough to secure it, then cut off the end of the straw so it doesn't show. Place the other "branch" on the side of the log, next to the top "bough," attach with the other piece of straw, and trim the straw. Frost the log and "branches" with the remaining frosting.

Decorate the log with the sugared rosemary and cranberries and/or moss. See page 196 for instructions.

The log can be stored in an airtight container in the refrigerator for up to 5 days.

WHIPPED ESPRESSO BUTTERCREAM | *Makes about 3½ cups*

¼ cup sifted all-purpose flour
1 cup whole milk
1½ teaspoons strong espresso (from a shot, or made from powdered espresso)
1 teaspoon pure vanilla extract
½ pound (2 sticks) unsalted butter, at room temperature
1 cup granulated sugar

Combine the flour, ¼ cup of the milk, the espresso, and vanilla in a small heavy saucepan and whisk until blended. Set the pan over medium heat and gradually add the remaining ¾ cup milk, whisking constantly, then cook, whisking, until the mixture comes to a low boil. Reduce the heat to low and whisk until the mixture begins to thicken and starts to "burp," 2 to 3 minutes.

Transfer the mixture to a small heatproof bowl and stir occasionally as it cools to keep it lump-free. If you do get a few lumps, don't worry—you can whisk the mixture to dissolve the lumps, or pass it through a fine-mesh sieve. (You can put the mixture in the refrigerator for 10 minutes to speed up the process.)

In the bowl of a stand mixer fitted with the whisk attachment (or in a large mixing bowl, using a handheld mixer), beat the butter on medium for 3 minutes, until soft and creamy. Gradually add the sugar and then beat on high speed for 5 to 7 minutes until the mixture is light and fluffy.

Reduce the speed and gradually add the milk mixture, then beat on medium-high speed for 4 to 5 minutes until thick and creamy.

Use immediately. Or store in an airtight container in the refrigerator for up to 3 days. To use buttercream that has been chilled, see the Tip on page 186.

CREATIVE DECORATIONS FOR YOUR YULE LOG

Holiday season means it's time to gild the lily—pull out all the stops.

SUGARED ROSEMARY AND CRANBERRIES

Combine ¾ cup granulated sugar and ½ cup water in a small saucepan and bring to a boil over medium heat.

Stir to dissolve the sugar. Set aside to cool.

Once the syrup is cool, drop in about 4 fresh rosemary sprigs and 1 cup cranberries, then remove with a slotted spoon, draining them well. Roll in extra-fine sugar, and sprinkle a little more sugar on top too. Spread out on a cookie sheet lined with parchment and set aside to dry for at least 2 hours. The extra sugar will crystallize in clumps just like snow. Store, uncovered, at room temperature for up to 4 days.

PISTACHIO MOSS

Put ¼ cup shelled pistachios in a small blender or coffee grinder and pulse until they look like powdery "moss." Store in an airtight container in the refrigerator for up to 2 weeks or freeze for up to 1 month.

Pull out the sparkly dragées, edible fresh flowers, and gum paste decorations too and decorate your Yule Log.

KEEPSAKE CAKE TOPPER

I think handmade gifts are the very best of all. I love the idea that this cake topper will help someone celebrate a special day and then become a timeless treasure to cherish. After the party is over, the honored guest will have a keepsake box for special mementos. I originally made this topper for a tiered celebration cake (see page 164) for a Sweet 16 party, but you can create one to celebrate all sorts of occasions, from graduations and birthdays to anniversaries and weddings. Instead of making numbers for these, add a vintage family photo or cut out other shapes, like silhouettes and hearts. *Makes 1 cake topper*

MATERIALS

4- to 5-inch round cardboard box with lid

Gold leaf sizing or liquid adhesive

Gold and silver leaf

About 40 inches 0.5-mm wire

50 to 100 tiny (4- to 5-mm) wooden beads

Pink and white acrylic paint (or other colors as desired)

Silver foil paper

Vintage trim

TOOLS

Paintbrush

Pencil

Wire cutters

Needle-nose pliers

Small paintbrush

Scissors

Hot glue gun

Step 1: Put your box and cover on your work surface. Using a paintbrush (follow the directions on the package of sizing), apply gold leaf sizing to the exterior of the box and lid. Let the sizing dry.

Step 2: Apply the gold and silver leaf with a paintbrush, transferring one piece at a time to the surface of the box and lid. For this topper, I tore the gold and silver leaf into small pieces and applied them randomly for a confetti-like appearance.

Step 3: Draw the number or numbers you want to create on a piece of scrap paper, approximately 3 to 4 inches in size. Loosely trace the numbers with 0.5-mm wire and cut to size using wire cutters. Straighten the wire and, using needle-nose pliers, curl one end of the piece of wire. Then thread tiny wooden beads onto the wire until it is filled and curl the end to secure them. Twist and bend the wire into the shape of the number. Repeat the process if making a second number.

Step 4: Using a small paintbrush, paint the beads as you desire with pink and white acrylic paint. To create an ombré effect, start with pink paint and slowly add white, working your way from one end of the number to the other. Allow to dry.

Step 5: Using the circumference of the box as a guide, measure out a hoop of wire for the arch and cut the wire to size. Using scissors, cut three 12-by-1½-inch strips of foil paper. Carefully fringe one edge of each strip, leaving a ¼-inch border. Straighten the wire, add a bead of hot glue to one end, and attach the first fringe strip, placing the unfringed edge at the tip. Once the glue is dry, twirl the wire, wrapping the fringe tightly and securing with glue as necessary. Add the remaining strips, completely covering the wire. Trim any excess fringe and reshape the wire into a hoop, leaving the ends open.

Step 6: Using the circumference of the box lid as a guide, measure out a piece of vintage trim and cut it to size. Use hot glue to secure it around the outside edge of the lid.

Step 7: With a pencil, mark the ideal spot for your numbers in the center of the box lid. Using hot glue, attach the numbers.

Step 8: Using the pencil, mark the placement for the fringed arch and then glue it into place. Your cake topper is ready.

SATURDAY SUPPER CLUB

SAVORY PIES AND COBBLERS, AND PIZZA

Throughout my childhood, I always looked forward to weekends, because that was when my parents opened up our home to family and friends. The ultimate compliment is when you have gatherings in your home and you can't seem to get anyone to leave! In fact, sometimes my parents' closest friends would show up with a bottle of wine and a suitcase on Friday, enjoy Saturday's supper club, and not leave until Sunday afternoon.

Entertaining has always been a significant part of my life. I grew up learning the essential ingredients for throwing a great party and playing hostess at a young age. These days, the bakery is our home-away-from-home, so once a month, we do a pop-up supper club—any excuse to unfold my vintage linens, and I'm in!

Our sign-up sheet fills up quickly, with everyone from some of our favorite regulars to visitors passing through Savannah on a trip. The bakery becomes a magical place after hours, the perfect setting for an evening of fun. Our vintage chandeliers are all aglow, and the tables are dressed up with flowers and tablecloths to make the affair a memorable evening. The supper club is a great excuse to cook our favorite comfort foods and to try new recipes, many of which you will find on the following pages.

After a long week of baking, we keep the supper club menu simple and serve family-style meals, with dishes that can be made in advance, like the Sweet Potato Potpie (page 202), Beans and Corn Bread Cobbler (page 204), and Tomato Pie (page 207). We always make sure to have a few snacks too, like the Candied Spiced Walnuts (page 220), or maybe our Devilish Eggs (page 222). One of my favorite serving ideas for a casual get-together is to set up interactive food stations like the Corn Bread Crostini Station (see page 224) with a variety of toppings. Setting up the food so that people can interact with both it and with each other is a great way to relax your guests and encourage conversation.

Even if your life is sometimes chaotic, don't be afraid to plan a gathering to catch up with friends. Getting everyone to pitch in will lighten your load and make it an easy affair for you to host. Put someone in charge of cocktails, including mocktails (see page 292). Enlist someone else to set the table and arrange the flowers. And encourage your friends to invite people you don't know—it's a great way to bring new faces into your social circle.

SWEET POTATO POTPIE

Serves 6

Potpies are one of my favorite comfort foods. A mix of sweet potato, corn, and Georgia butter peas goes into the filling for this one, which is topped with our flaky piecrust. It's a hearty recipe you can serve when your vegetarian friends come over for dinner.

FOR THE VEGETABLES

3 tablespoons unsalted butter
1 large sweet potato, peeled and cut into ½-inch cubes
2 celery ribs, cut into ½-inch pieces
1 medium sweet onion, finely chopped
1 cup corn kernels
1 cup cooked butter peas or butter beans
2 garlic cloves, minced
¼ teaspoon fine sea salt
¼ teaspoon freshly ground black pepper

FOR THE CREAM SAUCE

8 tablespoons (1 stick) unsalted butter
½ cup unbleached all-purpose flour
1 teaspoon rubbed sage (see Tip, page 45)
¼ teaspoon freshly grated nutmeg
¼ teaspoon fine sea salt
¼ teaspoon freshly ground black pepper

2½ cups vegetable stock
½ cup heavy cream

1 recipe Extra-Flaky Piecrust (page 120)
1 large egg, lightly beaten with a pinch of fine sea salt for egg wash

SPECIAL EQUIPMENT

Six 6-inch oven-proof bowls

To prepare the vegetables: Melt the butter in a large saucepan over medium heat. Add the sweet potato and sauté for 3 to 4 minutes. Add the celery, onion, corn, butter peas, garlic, salt, and pepper and sauté for 5 minutes, or until all the vegetables are slightly tender. Transfer the vegetables to a large bowl. Set aside.

To make the cream sauce: Melt the butter in a large saucepan over medium heat. Sprinkle the flour over the butter and cook, whisking, until a smooth paste forms. Whisk in the rubbed sage, grated nutmeg, fine sea salt, pepper, vegetable stock, and heavy cream and cook, whisking, until the sauce thickens slightly.

Pour the cream sauce over the vegetable mixture and stir to combine.

Position a rack in the middle of the oven and preheat the oven to 375°F. Place six 6-inch ovenproof bowls on a baking sheet.

On a lightly floured surface, using a rolling pin, roll one disk of dough out to a ¼-inch thickness. Put one of the bowls upside down on the dough as a guide and, using a knife, cut a circle 1 inch larger in diameter than the bowl. Cut out 2 more circles of the same size. Roll out the second disk of dough and cut out 3 more circles.

Divide the vegetables among the bowls, filling them about three-quarters full. Lay the dough rounds over the tops of the bowls, making sure the dough hangs evenly over the edges, and press to seal. Brush the dough with the egg wash. Cut a few slits in the tops of each pie with a sharp knife.

Bake the potpies for 20 to 25 minutes, until the crust is golden brown. Serve immediately.

BEANS AND CORN BREAD COBBLER

Serves 8

A catchy tune called "Beans and Corn Bread" pops into my head whenever we prepare this dish. It's one of those songs that once you hear it, it sticks. Like the song, this meal is one that sticks too . . . to your ribs. Soft butter beans, smoky bacon, and sweet, tender corn bread make me want to sing, "Beans and corn bread—outta sight!"

FOR THE BEANS
2 tablespoons olive oil
6 slices thick-cut applewood smoked bacon, cut into ¼-inch pieces
1½ cups cubed (½-inch pieces) sweet onions
2 large garlic cloves, minced
1 tablespoon chopped fresh sage
4 cups cooked butter beans

1 cup cubed (½-inch pieces) tomatoes
1 cup chicken stock
6 tablespoons brown sugar
1 tablespoon chopped fresh thyme
Fine sea salt and freshly ground black pepper

FOR THE CORN BREAD
1½ cups yellow cornmeal
½ cup unbleached all-purpose flour

¼ cup granulated sugar
2 teaspoons baking powder, preferably aluminum-free
2 teaspoons fine sea salt
1 teaspoon freshly ground black pepper
½ teaspoon baking soda
2 cups buttermilk
2 large eggs, lightly beaten
2 tablespoons unsalted butter, melted

Position a rack in the middle of the oven and preheat the oven to 400°F.

To prepare the beans: Put the olive oil and bacon in a 10-inch cast-iron skillet and cook over medium-high heat, stirring, until the bacon is cooked but not crisp, 5 to 6 minutes. Add the onions, garlic, and sage and cook until the onions are soft, about 3 minutes.

Add the butter beans, tomatoes, chicken stock, brown sugar, and thyme and bring to a boil, then reduce the heat and simmer, stirring occasionally, until the liquid reduces and thickens, 10 to 12 minutes. Add salt and pepper to taste, remove from the heat, and set aside.

To prepare the corn bread: In a large bowl, combine the cornmeal, flour, sugar, baking powder, salt, pepper, and baking soda and stir well. Add the buttermilk, eggs, and butter and stir until just combined. It's okay if the batter looks lumpy; do not overmix. Pour the batter into the skillet over the beans and spread it to the edges of the pan.

Place the skillet in the oven and bake for 20 to 25 minutes, until the top of the corn bread is golden brown. Let stand for 5 to 10 minutes before serving.

TOMATO PIE

Serves 8

At the peak of tomato season, we're canning, roasting, or eating them as fast as we can. This is one of our favorite recipes to put sweet fresh tomatoes to use. If you don't have the space or time to grow your own, use the highest-quality tomatoes you can find. We love heirloom tomatoes for their flavor and beautiful colors, which make this pie appealing to the eye as well as to your taste buds.

3 cups diced seeded heirloom tomatoes, plus 2 cups cubed (1-inch pieces) seeded tomatoes
2 teaspoons fine sea salt, or to taste
1 teaspoon granulated sugar, or to taste
4 tablespoons unsalted butter

4 medium sweet onions, thinly sliced
2 teaspoons balsamic vinegar
2 cups halved heirloom cherry tomatoes
2 tablespoons olive oil
1 tablespoon fresh thyme leaves
¾ cup mayonnaise

⅓ cup finely grated Parmigiano-Reggiano cheese
⅓ cup coarsely grated Fontina cheese
½ cup chopped fresh basil
Freshly ground black pepper

1 parbaked Extra-Flaky Piecrust (page 120), cooled

Put the diced tomatoes in a bowl, add ½ teaspoon of the salt and the sugar, and toss well. Transfer the tomatoes to a sieve set over a bowl and let them drain for 1 hour. Give them a toss every 20 minutes to speed up the draining.

Meanwhile, melt the butter in a large skillet over medium-high heat. Add the onions, season with 1 teaspoon of the salt, and cook, stirring occasionally, until tender and translucent, about 15 minutes. Reduce the heat to low and let the onions slowly caramelize, stirring occasionally, until they turn a medium brown color, 30 to 40 minutes. Remove from the heat, stir in the balsamic vinegar, and let cool to room temperature.

Position a rack in the middle of the oven and preheat the oven to 350°F. Line two baking sheets with parchment.

While the onions cook, in a medium bowl, toss the cubed and cherry tomatoes with the olive oil, the remaining ½ teaspoon salt, and the thyme. Spread the tomatoes in a single layer on the prepared baking sheets and roast for 20 to 30 minutes, until caramelized but not burnt. Set aside.

In a medium bowl, combine the mayonnaise and the two cheeses, mixing well.

continued

In a large bowl, combine the drained tomatoes, roasted tomatoes, caramelized onions, and basil. Tomatoes often need a good dose of seasoning to bring out the flavors: taste and add more salt and/or sugar and pepper to your liking.

Spread the tomato mixture evenly in the parbaked piecrust. Top with the mayo-cheese mixture, spreading it to about 1 inch from the edges, leaving a border so you can see the tomatoes. Bake for 20 to 25 minutes, until the top is golden brown. Serve warm.

The pie can be refrigerated, tightly covered, for up to 3 days. Reheat in a 350°F oven to serve.

FARMERS'-MARKET QUICHE

Serves 6

This recipe is one of the most flexible I know. Head to the farmers' market and pick whichever vegetables are in season and look best. You can easily exchange one vegetable for another to customize the recipe for the season. Roasting the vegetables before baking the quiche gives them a caramelized sweetness that heightens their flavors. Serve for brunch or for dinner with a small salad.

FOR THE FILLING
1 cup halved cherry tomatoes
½ cup cubed (½-inch pieces) peeled sweet potato
½ cup cubed (½-inch pieces) sweet onion
½ cup corn kernels
¼ cup diced jarred roasted red peppers
1 tablespoon olive oil
¼ teaspoon fine sea salt
¼ teaspoon freshly ground black pepper

FOR THE CUSTARD
3 large eggs
1 cup heavy cream
½ teaspoon fine sea salt
½ teaspoon smoked paprika
½ teaspoon dried thyme
¼ teaspoon freshly ground black pepper
⅛ teaspoon freshly grated nutmeg

¾ cup grated Gruyère cheese
1 parbaked Extra-Flaky Piecrust (page 120), cooled
8 large fresh basil leaves

Position a rack in the middle of the oven and preheat the oven to 400°F. Line a baking pan with parchment.

Put all the vegetables in a large bowl, add the olive oil, salt, and pepper, and toss to coat. Spread the vegetables evenly on the prepared baking sheet.

Roast the vegetables for 10 to 15 minutes, until the edges start to become charred. Let cool. Turn the oven temperature down to 325°F.

To make the custard: In a medium bowl, whisk the eggs to break them up. Add the cream, salt, smoked paprika, thyme, pepper, and nutmeg and whisk to combine.

Scatter ½ cup of the Gruyère over the bottom of the crust. Pour the custard over the cheese. Add the roasted vegetables, arranging them evenly, and top with the basil leaves and the remaining ¼ cup Gruyère.

Place the quiche on a baking sheet and bake for 30 to 40 minutes, until the center is set. Serve warm.

SPOON BREAD

Serves 8

"Simple to make and easy to please" is what my grandma Hannah would always say when serving this dish. Classic and traditional, spoon bread graces many a table in the South during the holidays. Although it's called spoon bread, it is more like a savory pudding or a soufflé.

2½ cups whole milk
½ teaspoon fine sea salt
½ cup fine yellow cornmeal

4 tablespoons unsalted
   butter, cubed
6 large eggs, separated
1 cup shredded sharp
   cheddar cheese

2 tablespoons dried
   marjoram
Butter, sorghum, and/or
   honey for serving

Position a rack in the middle of the oven and preheat the oven to 350°F. Lightly butter a 1½-quart baking dish.

Combine the milk and salt in a medium saucepan and heat the milk over medium heat until small bubbles appear around the edges. Add the cornmeal, whisking constantly, reduce the heat to medium-low, and cook, whisking, until the mixture thickens, about 4 minutes. Add the butter and stir to melt and combine. Remove from the heat, transfer to a large bowl, and let cool slightly, about 10 minutes.

In the bowl of a stand mixer fitted with the whisk attachment (or in a large bowl, using a handheld mixer), beat the egg whites on medium-high speed until stiff peaks form.

Whisk the egg yolks one at a time into the cornmeal mixture, mixing well. Add the cheese and marjoram and stir to combine. Using a rubber spatula, gently fold in one-third of the egg whites until barely combined. Fold in the rest of the egg whites, working quickly but being careful not to deflate the egg whites. Phew! I love how this dish comes together.

Pour the batter into the prepared baking dish and smooth the top. Bake for 45 minutes, or until the top is golden brown. Serve warm, with butter, sorghum, and/or honey.

PIZZA THE DAY WAY

Makes four 12-inch pizzas

Saturday night is our time for pizza. We mix the dough the night before and refrigerate it until we're ready to use it; refrigerating the dough overnight allows it to develop great flavor, and it gives you the opportunity to plan ahead too. Making pizza for the family is fun, and having the option to customize your own toppings is even more fun.

4½ cups unbleached all-purpose flour
2 teaspoons fine sea salt
½ teaspoon instant yeast

1¾ cups water

Toppings of your choice; see the Sweet Note

OPTIONAL SPECIAL EQUIPMENT
Baking stone
Pizza pan

In the bowl of a stand mixer fitted with the dough hook, combine the flour, salt, and yeast. Turn the mixer on to low speed, add the water, and mix until the dough comes together. Turn the speed up to medium and mix for 3 to 5 minutes, until a smooth, elastic dough forms.

Transfer the dough to an oiled bowl, turning to coat the dough with oil. Cover the bowl with plastic wrap and refrigerate for 24 hours. (At this point, you have the option to freeze the dough for future use: Divide the dough into 4 equal pieces and shape each one into a ball. Wrap in plastic wrap and then aluminum foil and freeze for up to 1 month. Thaw in the refrigerator for 24 to 48 hours.)

Remove the dough from the refrigerator and divide into 4 equal pieces. Shape each piece into a tight ball, pinching the bottom seams closed, and arrange on a baking sheet. Put back into the refrigerator to rest for 4 hours.

Meanwhile, at least 1 hour before you are ready to bake, position a rack in the middle of the oven and put a baking stone on the rack. (If you don't have a stone, bake the pizza on a pizza pan or a baking sheet.) Preheat the oven to 450°F.

When you're ready to make pizza, remove as many pieces of dough from the refrigerator as you want to bake and allow to rest for about 30 minutes.

To shape each pizza, coat the ball of dough with flour and, working on a lightly floured work surface, press and stretch with your fingers, working from the center out to the edges, to form into a 12-inch round. Top with your choice of ingredients.

Bake on the baking stone (or pizza pan or baking sheet) for 12 to 15 minutes. Cut into slices and serve.

PIZZA TOPPING IDEAS

Top your own individual pizza with the ingredients you like most. Here are some of our favorite combinations; go ahead and try them or create your own.

Tomato sauce, pepperoni, sliced Peppadew peppers, shredded Pecorino Romano cheese, fresh basil, and olive oil

Shredded Fontina cheese, Vidalia Onion Marmalade (page 272), sliced scallions, olive oil, and flaky sea salt

Shredded Provolone cheese, roasted tomatoes, Pickled Red Onions (page 277), Italian seasoning, freshly ground black pepper, and olive oil

BUTTERMILK WAFFLES WITH CANDIED BACON

In my book, waffles are one of those foods that can be eaten any time of day. Although they are traditionally eaten at breakfast, alongside some bacon and eggs, here we put the bacon *inside*, adding savory bits to every bite. We love to serve these waffles for dinner, nestled up to some crispy fried chicken.

Makes 6 to 8 waffles

FOR THE CANDIED BACON

10 slices thick-cut applewood-smoked bacon
¼ cup maple syrup
⅓ cup packed light brown sugar

FOR THE WAFFLES

2 cups unbleached all-purpose flour
¼ cup packed light brown sugar
1½ teaspoons baking powder, preferably aluminum-free
1 teaspoon baking soda
½ teaspoon ground cinnamon
½ teaspoon fine sea salt
¼ teaspoon ground ginger
3 large eggs, separated, at room temperature
2 cups buttermilk, at room temperature
8 tablespoons (1 stick) unsalted butter, melted
1 teaspoon pure vanilla extract

Maple syrup for serving

To make the candied bacon: Preheat the oven to 350°F. Line a baking sheet with aluminum foil.

Line up the bacon slices side by side on the prepared baking sheet. Brush both sides of each piece with maple syrup and cover both sides with brown sugar.

Bake for 10 minutes. Turn the bacon over and bake for an additional 4 to 6 minutes, until cooked through. Remove from the oven and place on a sheet of parchment to cool.

When the bacon is cool, roughly chop it into ½-inch pieces. Set aside.

To make the waffles: Preheat a waffle iron and grease with a little butter or nonstick spray. Meanwhile, in a large bowl, whisk together the flour, sugar, baking powder, baking soda, cinnamon, salt, and ginger. Add the candied bacon bits and stir to combine.

continued

In a medium bowl, whisk together the egg yolks, buttermilk, melted butter, and vanilla.

In the bowl of a stand mixer fitted with the whisk attachment (or in a medium bowl, using a handheld mixer), beat the egg whites until soft peaks form.

Add the egg yolk mixture to the flour mixture and mix well. Fold in the egg whites.

To cook the waffles: For each waffle, ladle about ⅓ cup of the batter onto the waffle maker, spreading it almost to the edges. Close the lid and cook for 3 to 5 minutes, or according to the manufacturer's instructions. Serve warm, with maple syrup.

CHIVE PARMIGIANO-REGGIANO POPOVERS

Popovers are light, airy pockets of goodness and they are a snap to make, requiring just a few ingredients. They can be mixed, baked, and put on the table in very little time. Keep in mind that it's okay if the batter is a little lumpy; avoid overmixing, and the batter will smooth out as it bakes.

Makes 12 small popovers

3 large eggs, at room temperature

1½ cups whole milk, at room temperature

1½ cups unbleached all-purpose flour

1¼ teaspoons flaky sea salt, such as Jacobsen or Maldon

2 tablespoons finely chopped fresh chives

¼ cup finely grated Parmigiano-Reggiano cheese

Butter for serving

SPECIAL EQUIPMENT
Nonstick mini popover pan (with 12 cups)

Position a rack in the lower third of the oven and preheat the oven to 450°F. Put a nonstick mini popover pan in the oven to preheat.

In a large bowl, vigorously whisk the eggs and milk until frothy, about 1 minute. Add the flour and salt and stir just until incorporated (there will still be some small lumps in the batter, and that's fine). Stir in the chives and cheese.

Remove the hot popover pan from the oven and spray it with nonstick spray.

Fill each popover cup two-thirds full with batter.

Bake the popovers for 15 minutes, then reduce the oven temperature to 350°F and continue to bake for another 20 to 25 minutes, until golden brown. Remove the pan from the oven and transfer the popovers to a wire rack. With a small knife, cut a hole in the side of each popover; this will allow the steam to escape and prevent the popovers from collapsing.

Popovers are best eaten while they are still warm, with a dab or two of butter.

CANDIED SPICED WALNUTS

We love to serve a batch of these nuts to a gathering of friends, when the family is over for the holidays, or for a weekend snack while watching the game.

Makes 4 cups

4 cups walnuts
¼ cup packed light brown
   sugar
2 teaspoons fine sea salt

1 teaspoon rubbed sage
   (see Tip, page 45)
½ teaspoon cayenne
   pepper

¼ teaspoon ground
   cinnamon
¼ cup olive oil
1 tablespoon honey

Position a rack in the middle of the oven and preheat the oven to 350°F. Line two baking sheets with parchment.

Put the nuts in a large bowl.

In a small bowl, whisk together the brown sugar, salt, sage, cayenne, and cinnamon. In a medium bowl, vigorously whisk the olive oil and honey until combined, about 1 minute.

Add the oil mixture to the nuts and toss to coat evenly. Add the sugar mixture and toss to coat evenly.

Spread the nuts out in a single layer in the prepared baking sheets. Bake for 8 minutes. Toss and stir the nuts and bake for another 4 minutes. Remove from the oven and let cool completely.

Stored in an airtight container, the nuts will keep for up to 2 weeks.

PIMENTO CHEESE

Makes about 6 cups

We are addicted to what is affectionately known as the caviar of the South. Our kicked-up version of pimento cheese gets a little twist from smoked paprika and bourbon. You can put it on crackers and eat a batch of it all by yourself, though you might feel a little better if you eat it with some crunchy vegetables too. Put it in a sandwich along with some bacon, and you've got one of the bakery's most popular sandwiches (see page 144).

1 pound sharp white cheddar cheese

¼ pound Pecorino Romano

½ cup mayonnaise, preferably Duke's

1 small garlic clove, crushed and minced

1½ teaspoons Kentucky bourbon

1 teaspoon stone-ground mustard

½ teaspoon smoked paprika

¼ to ½ teaspoon cayenne pepper, or to taste

½ cup diced pimentos

Using the large holes on a box grater, shred the cheddar and Pecorino Romano cheese. Transfer the cheese to a medium bowl and toss to combine.

In a small bowl, combine the mayonnaise, garlic, bourbon, mustard, paprika, and cayenne and stir to mix well.

Add the mayonnaise mixture and pimentos to the bowl of cheese and gently toss to combine.

Cover the bowl tightly with plastic wrap and refrigerate for 8 to 12 hours, to let the flavors come together.

The pimento cheese can be refrigerated for up to 1 week.

DEVILISH EGGS

*Makes
24 stuffed
eggs*

I always know it's going to be a great party if I see a plate of deviled eggs on the buffet. They are a staple at parties here in the South. At our house, you'll find them sitting pretty, right next to the Pimento Cheese Crackers (page 146). I like my deviled eggs made with plenty of sweet pickle relish, topped with a garnish of tomato and onion and just a sprinkle of paprika. You can be creative and try other toppings too, like diced pimentos, capers, or chopped fresh thyme or flat-leaf parsley. Our friend Angie named these devilish eggs, because they are just so darn good you can't resist them!

12 hard-boiled eggs (see the Sweet Note)

6 tablespoons mayonnaise, preferably Duke's

3 tablespoons sour cream

1 tablespoon sweet pickle relish

1 tablespoon Dijon mustard

⅛ teaspoon cayenne pepper (optional)

Freshly ground black pepper

2 cherry tomatoes, each cut into 12 pieces

1 scallion, minced

Flaky sea salt, such as Jacobsen or Maldon

Smoked paprika for garnish

Slice the hard-boiled eggs crosswise in half. Gently scoop the yolks into a medium bowl. Trim a tiny bit off the bottom of each egg white half so that they will sit upright. Set the egg whites aside on a serving dish, waiting to be filled.

Add the mayonnaise, sour cream, pickle relish, Dijon mustard, cayenne, if using, and black pepper to taste to the egg yolks. Gently mix until smooth and creamy.

Using a spoon, a small scoop, or a pastry bag, fill each egg white half with some of the yolk mixture. Top each egg with a piece of tomato, a few pieces of scallion, and a sprinkle of sea salt.

Cover loosely with plastic wrap and refrigerate until party time.

Just before serving, using a fine-mesh sieve, lightly dust the filling in each egg with smoked paprika.

Tip: You can make the deviled eggs a day in advance and keep them refrigerated. Never leave them out at room temperature for more than 2 hours.

HOW TO MAKE THE PERFECT HARD-BOILED EGGS

I know you're thinking, *Who doesn't know how to boil an egg?* But I used to boil my eggs until they were overcooked and green on the inside. In one of my many calls home to my mom, I learned how to do it the right way. Here is Janie Queen's method for the perfect hard-boiled egg.

Put the eggs in a saucepan large enough to hold them in a single layer. Add cold water to cover the eggs by 1 to 2 inches and add salt (1 tablespoon per 6 eggs). Bring to a rolling boil over high heat. Remove from the heat, cover the pan with a lid, and let the eggs stand for 12 minutes if using large eggs, 15 minutes for extra-large eggs.

Carefully pour off the hot water, cover the eggs with cold water, and let stand for about 20 minutes. And, just like that, you'll have perfectly hard-boiled eggs. Drain, peel, and set on paper towels to dry.

SET UP A CROSTINI* STATION FOR YOUR SUPPER CLUB

My sister, Natalie, was my entertaining guru. She had a knack for taking casual get-togethers to another level. She would set up the most clever interactive food stations; hers were the inspiration for my crostini station. Here's how we do it Southern style.

Bake a pan of corn bread (see page 204), in a (sprayed and parchment-lined) baking sheet so you get thin corn bread, at 400°F for 18 to 20 minutes, or until the top is golden. Once the corn bread has cooled, cut it into 2-inch rounds, or into any shape you like, using a 2-inch cookie cutter. Line two baking sheets with parchment and place the little corn bread rounds on the pans. Toast them in a 350°F oven for about 5 minutes to make crostini. (Of course, you could also pick up some baguettes from your favorite bakery, slice them, and toast those up.)

Set a table with your favorite linens and decorate with some pretty flowers. Set out assorted bowls, platters, and bread boards on the table to create variety. Put the crostini toasts in two baskets at opposite ends of the table, with a stack of plates next to each. I like to make little menu banners, using two paper straws or skewers to secure them to the baskets, that say "Make Your Own Crostini—Be Creative."

Fill the bowls and platters with cured meats and cheeses; marinated olives; olive oil with salt and pepper (and other spices such as fennel pollen); pickled and roasted vegetables; and some homemade condiments, like Vidalia Onion Marmalade (page 272), Pimento Cheese (page 221), and Lemon Butter Bean Spread (page 278). Don't forget the Devilish Eggs (page 222). Finally, make up a tray with a few of your favorite crostini combinations to get the ball rolling.

*That's a fancy Italian term for little toasts with toppings!

LUNCH CANISTER

I remember when choosing a lunch box was one of the most exciting things about back-to-school shopping. But who says you can't still get a thrill from a lunch box? This lunch canister brings the cool back into packing a lunch, and I'll show you how to give yours a personality all its own by repurposing a vintage canister, and maybe even a vintage belt, to make it. This project calls for a bit of foraging in thrift shops (Etsy and eBay are great online sources), along with a few simple tools.

When it's time to pack your lunch, I recommend using small storage containers (BPA-free, of course) and/or Snack Pockets (page 149) to keep foods separate and fresh. This lunch container is also great for food gifts. Once the goodies are gone, the canister lives on as a multifunctional container to enjoy day after day. *Makes 1 canister*

MATERIALS
Vintage metal canister (from flour, sugar, tea, etc.) with a lid
2 grommet sets
Leather strap or vintage belt

TOOLS
Grommet punch and setter, such as the Crop-a-Dile Eyelet and Punch Kit
Scissors
Pencil

Step 1: Wash and dry the metal canister and the lid. Leave the lid off for now.

Step 2: Using a grommet punch, punch two holes side by side on two opposite sides of the container. The thickness of the leather strap or belt will determine the distance between the holes; make sure the holes won't interfere with the lid.

Step 3: The leather strap or belt will be the handle of your lunch box. Decide how long you want to make it and cut the strap or belt to size.

Step 4: Hold the leather over the two sets of holes and mark the leather accordingly with a pencil, then punch holes into the leather.

Step 5: Using the grommets and setting tool, check to make sure the handle is secure. Put the lid on, and your lunch pail is ready for use. Attach the leather strap to the canister.

A SATISFYING TREAT SAVES THE DAY

COOKIES, BROWNIES, AND BARS

The pulse of the bakery beats fast on weekends when it is jam-packed with folks dropping by to gather, eat, and linger while enjoying our Southern-inspired sweets and savory bites. I still find the most joy when I see families stopping in for an afternoon treat. I love seeing the children press their faces against our glass cases to get a closer look at all the goodies inside.

One of my favorite moments happened on a recent busy Saturday afternoon. When the dining room is buzzing like this, I like to walk through the bakery to say hi to our guests and friends. On that day, I heard the tiniest voice rise above the clamor, calling my name. Drawing out every syllable, she said, "Hiiiiiii, Miss Cher-rrryl." I looked over and saw one of my favorite customers sitting with her mom, with an enormous cookie that she could barely hold and an even bigger smile on her face. I sat for a few minutes to chat with her about her day and her "yummy" snack. She was very happy that I took a moment to visit with her, and so was I.

It's treasured moments like these that make my day and remind me of why Griff and I wake up so darn early in the morning to bake. I can still get choked up every time I connect with a young customer like this, because not only does it take me back to my own Saturday visits to Blum's Bakery in Los Angeles with my dad, it also inspires me to make sure we continue to build relationships that allow folks to create their own stories in our bakery.

This chapter includes some of our customers' most-loved afternoon snacks and lunch-box treats, including some that little hands often point to, like the PB&J Sammies (page 250), Chocolate Cream Sammies (page 241), Decorated Sugar Cookies (page 246), and Marshmallow–Chocolate Cookie Sammies (page 243). But grown-ups like snacks too. Star Brownies (page 234), Brown Sugar–Chocolate Chip Shortbread (page 235), and Cornmeal Jam Drops (page 240) make an afternoon cup of coffee or tea even better. Snack time is a great time of day for everyone—not just kids.

OLD-FASHIONED SUGAR COOKIES

This sugar cookie is simple, buttery, and delicate, with just a hint of lemon zest. Sugar cookies pack well, making them the ideal lunch-box treat.

Makes about 12 cookies

2 cups unbleached all-purpose flour
½ teaspoon baking soda
¼ teaspoon fine sea salt
8 tablespoons (1 stick) unsalted butter, at room temperature

½ cup canola oil
½ cup granulated sugar, plus extra for sprinkling
½ cup confectioners' sugar
1 large egg
2 teaspoons pure vanilla extract

Grated zest of 1 small lemon

Position a rack in the middle of the oven and preheat the oven to 350°F. Line a cookie sheet with parchment.

In a large mixing bowl, whisk together the flour, baking soda, and salt. Set aside.

In the bowl of a stand mixer fitted with the paddle attachment (or in a large mixing bowl, using a handheld mixer), beat the butter on medium speed for about 1 minute, until creamy. Add the canola oil, mixing until incorporated, then add the granulated sugar and confectioners' sugar, mixing well. One at a time, add the egg, vanilla, and lemon zest, mixing until incorporated.

With the mixer on low, add the dry ingredients, beating until just combined.

Remove the bowl from the mixer and finish mixing by hand to make sure no bits of flour or butter are hiding on the bottom of the bowl and the dough is thoroughly mixed. Cover with plastic wrap and place in the freezer for 15 minutes (or in the refrigerator for about 1 hour) to make the dough easier to scoop.

Use a small ice cream scoop to form the cookies, about 1 rounded tablespoon each, and place on the prepared cookie sheet, leaving 2 inches between them to allow for spreading. With the palm of your hand, flatten each cookie to a ¼-inch thickness. Sprinkle the tops liberally with granulated sugar.

Bake the cookies for 8 to 10 minutes, rotating the pan halfway through the baking time, until the edges are lightly golden. Let cool completely on a wire rack.

The cookies can be stored in an airtight container at room temperature for up to 3 days.

HONEY OAT COOKIES

Makes 12 cookies

You mix the dough for these cookies by hand, without having to use an electric mixer. What could be easier? Our customers rationalize that the large amount of oatmeal in the cookie makes it good for you, and I agree. All the ingredients come together to make a soft, chewy cookie with lots of flavor.

1 cup old-fashioned rolled oats (not quick-cooking)
1¼ cups sweetened flaked coconut
¼ cup packed light brown sugar
¾ cup unbleached all-purpose flour

1 teaspoon baking soda
½ teaspoon ground cinnamon
8 tablespoons (1 stick) unsalted butter, cut into chunks
1 tablespoon honey
1 tablespoon water

1 teaspoon pure vanilla extract

FOR THE CHOCOLATE TOPPING
½ cup semisweet chocolate chips
1 teaspoon vegetable oil
Pinch of fine sea salt

Position a rack in the middle of the oven and preheat the oven to 350°F. Line a cookie sheet with parchment.

In a large bowl, whisk the oats, coconut, brown sugar, flour, baking soda, and cinnamon together thoroughly. Set aside.

In a small saucepan, combine the butter, honey, water, and vanilla and heat over medium-low heat, stirring, until the butter is melted and the mixture is thoroughly combined. Remove from the heat.

Make a well in the center of the flour mixture and pour in the butter mixture. Using a rubber spatula, fold the butter mixture thoroughly into the flour mixture and let sit for 5 minutes.

Use a small ice cream scoop to form the cookies, about 2 rounded tablespoons each, and place on the prepared cookie sheet, leaving 1 inch between them. With the palm of your hand, flatten each cookie into a 3-inch round, about ½ inch thick.

Bake the cookies for 10 to 12 minutes, rotating the pan halfway through the baking time, until they are a deep golden color. Let cool completely on a wire rack.

In a small pan, combine the chocolate chips, oil, and salt and heat over low heat, stirring constantly, until the chocolate is almost melted. Turn off the heat and stir until the chocolate is completely melted.Using a spoon, top each cookie with some of the topping. Let stand until the topping has set.

The cookies can be stored in an airtight container at room temperature for up to 5 days.

SMORGASBORD COOKIES

Makes about 24 cookies

These are packed with so many ingredients that they are like a smorgasbord in cookie form. Think of them as kicked-up chocolate chip cookies, with lots of mix-ins: a hefty amount of chocolate chunks, white chocolate chips, butterscotch chips, walnuts, potato chips, and pretzels. Trust me on this one—they're addictive.

2½ cups unbleached all-purpose flour
1¼ teaspoons baking soda
1¼ teaspoons fine sea salt
½ pound (2 sticks) unsalted butter, at room temperature

1 cup granulated sugar
1 cup packed light brown sugar
1 tablespoon molasses
1 teaspoon pure vanilla extract
2 large eggs, at room temperature

1 cup semisweet chocolate chunks
¾ cup white chocolate chips
¾ cup butterscotch chips
1 cup chopped walnuts
2 cups ruffled potato chips
1 cup mini pretzels

Line two cookie sheets with parchment.

In a large mixing bowl, whisk together the flour, baking soda, and salt. Set aside.

In the bowl of a stand mixer fitted with the paddle attachment (or in a large mixing bowl, using a handheld mixer), cream together the butter, both sugars, the molasses, and vanilla on medium-high speed for 2 to 3 minutes. Add the eggs and beat for 5 to 7 minutes, until very light and fluffy.

Turn the mixer speed down to low and add the dry ingredients in thirds, beating until combined. With the mixer running, one at a time, add the chocolate chunks, white chocolate chips, butterscotch chips, walnuts, potato chips, and pretzels. You want them to be in large, chunky pieces.

Use a large ice cream scoop or a ¼-cup measuring cup to form the cookies and place on the prepared cookie sheets, leaving 2 inches between them to allow for spreading. Lightly tap each cookie slightly with the palm of your hand to flatten it. Cover the cookie sheets with plastic wrap and refrigerate for at least 30 minutes, or for up to 3 days, before baking.

Position the racks in the middle and lower third of the oven and preheat the oven to 350°F.

Bake the cookies for 15 to 18 minutes, rotating the pans halfway through the baking time, until the edges are golden brown. Let the cookies cool completely on a wire rack.

The cookies can be stored in an airtight container at room temperature for up to 3 days.

BROWN SUGAR– CHOCOLATE CHIP SHORTBREAD

Makes about 24 cookies

Shortbread cookies are great time-savers. You can make the dough up to a month in advance—because it has a hefty amount of butter, it stays tender longer than most doughs. You can scoop it into cookies and let them set in the fridge for 30 minutes, then wrap them and freeze in an airtight container, ready to bake whenever the mood strikes.

½ pound (2 sticks) unsalted butter, at room temperature
1 cup packed light brown sugar
½ teaspoon fine sea salt

1½ teaspoons pure vanilla extract
2¼ cups unbleached all-purpose flour
½ cup mini semisweet chocolate chips

Granulated sugar for dusting if using a cookie stamp

OPTIONAL SPECIAL EQUIPMENT
Cookie stamp (see Resources, page 293)

Position the racks in the middle and lower third of the oven and preheat the oven to 350°F. Line two cookie sheets with parchment.

In the bowl of a stand mixer fitted with the paddle attachment (or in a large mixing bowl, using a handheld mixer), cream together the butter, brown sugar, salt, and vanilla on medium-high speed for 5 to 7 minutes, until very light and fluffy. Don't rush this step.

Add the flour in thirds, beating until incorporated. Add the chocolate chips and mix until just combined.

Use a small ice cream scoop to form the cookies, about 1 rounded tablespoon each, and place on the prepared cookie sheets, leaving 1 inch between them to allow for spreading. Flatten each cookie with a decorative cookie stamp dusted with granulated sugar, or lightly spray the bottom of a flat-bottomed measuring cup with nonstick spray and flatten the tops slightly.

Bake the cookies for 10 to 12 minutes, rotating the pans halfway through the baking time, until they are golden brown. (If you are baking cookies from the freezer, they will take a couple of minutes longer.) Let cool completely on a wire rack.

The cookies can be stored in an airtight container at room temperature for up to 3 days.

KEY LIME SHORTBREAD COOKIES

These shortbread cookies are loaded with enough lime flavor to make you pucker up. They have a delicate, buttery, melt-in-your-mouth texture and are topped with a glaze made with both lime juice and zest.

Makes 24 cookies

½ pound (2 sticks) unsalted butter, at room temperature
1 teaspoon pure vanilla extract
¼ teaspoon fine sea salt

Grated zest of 2 limes
1¼ cups confectioners' sugar
2 cups unbleached all-purpose flour

FOR THE GLAZE
¾ cup confectioners' sugar
Grated zest of 1 lime
2 tablespoons fresh lime juice

Line two cookie sheets with parchment.

In the bowl of a stand mixer fitted with the paddle attachment (or in a large mixing bowl, using a handheld mixer), cream together the butter, vanilla, salt, and lime zest on medium speed until combined. Turn the mixer speed down to low and add the confectioners' sugar, then mix on medium-high speed for 3 to 5 minutes, until very light and fluffy.

Add the flour in thirds, beating until just combined, no more than 2 minutes.

Use a small ice cream scoop to form the cookies, about 1 rounded tablespoon each, and place on the prepared cookie sheets, leaving 1 inch between them to allow for spreading. Lightly spray the bottom of a flat-bottomed measuring cup with nonstick spray and flatten the top of each cookie slightly. Refrigerate for at least 30 minutes, and up to 1 hour, before baking.

Position the racks in the middle and lower third of the oven and preheat the oven to 350°F.

Bake the cookies for 8 to 10 minutes, rotating the pans halfway through the baking time, until the edges are lightly golden. Let cool completely on a wire rack.

To make the glaze: Mix the confectioners' sugar, lime zest, and lime juice in a small bowl until smooth. Add water 1 teaspoon at a time if necessary to reach a nice spreading consistency.

Drop a dollop of glaze on each cookie and let set. The cookies can be stored in an airtight container for up to 3 days.

TYBEE SAND DOLLAR COOKIES

Makes about 24 cookies

Tybee Island, Georgia, is often referred to as Savannah's beach, and it is one of Griff's and my favorite weekend getaways. There is just something so rejuvenating about a quiet walk on a sandy beach. These light, delicate, and crumbly cookies have a sandy consistency, and they look a bit like sand dollars too.

½ pound (2 sticks) unsalted butter, at room temperature

⅓ cup granulated sugar

½ teaspoon fine sea salt

1 teaspoon pure vanilla extract

2 cups unbleached all-purpose flour

1 cup pecans, coarsely chopped

1 cup raw sugar

1 egg white, beaten for egg wash

In the bowl of a stand mixer fitted with the paddle attachment (or in a large mixing bowl, using a handheld mixer), cream together the butter, granulated sugar, salt, and vanilla on medium-high speed for 3 to 5 minutes, until very light and fluffy.

Add the flour in thirds, beating until just combined.

Remove the bowl from the mixer and fold in the pecans. Then finish mixing by hand.

Divide the dough in half. Roll each half into a 2-inch-thick log. Wrap in plastic wrap and freeze for 1 hour, or refrigerate overnight.

Position the racks in the middle and lower third of the oven and preheat the oven to 350°F. Line two cookie sheets with parchment.

Sprinkle the raw sugar over a piece of parchment. Brush each log with the egg wash and roll in the sugar, pressing slightly as you roll to make sure that it is covered completely.

Slice the logs into ½-inch-thick slices and arrange on the prepared cookie sheets, leaving about 1 inch between them to allow for spreading.

Bake the cookies for 12 to 14 minutes, rotating the pans halfway through the baking time, until they are golden brown. Let cool completely on a wire rack.

The cookies can be stored in an airtight container at room temperature for up to 3 days.

CORNMEAL JAM DROPS

Makes about 24 cookies

After a long day of baking, Griff and I have a ritual of enjoying a cup of tea and a cookie or two in the late afternoon. This cookie always makes it to my plate. It's tender and buttery and slightly crisp on the edges, with just the right amount of sweetness from the jam in the center. You can customize it with your favorite fillings if you like. Try the Lemon Curd (see page 172) as the filling for a tart twist.

1 large egg, at room temperature

1 teaspoon pure vanilla extract

1¼ cups unbleached all-purpose flour

½ cup almond flour

½ cup confectioners' sugar

½ cup yellow cornmeal

Grated zest of 1 lemon

½ teaspoon fine sea salt

¼ teaspoon ground cardamom

8 tablespoons (1 stick) cold unsalted butter, cut into cubes

⅔ cup Raspberry Jam (page 266), Blackberry Lime Jam (page 269), or any favorite flavor

In a small bowl, whisk together the egg and vanilla. Set aside.

In the bowl of a stand mixer fitted with the paddle attachment (or in a large mixing bowl, using a handheld mixer), combine the two flours, the confectioners' sugar, cornmeal, lemon zest, salt, and cardamom and mix on low speed to blend. Add the cubed butter a few pieces at a time, mixing until the mixture resembles coarse meal. Add the egg and vanilla and mix for 1 minute.

Scrape the dough onto a lightly floured surface and form into a ball. Wrap in plastic wrap, then flatten with the palm of your hand to form a disk. Place the dough in the refrigerator for at least 1 hour to chill, or for up to 2 weeks.

Position a rack in the middle of the oven and preheat the oven to 375°F. Line two cookie sheets with parchment.

Use a small ice cream scoop to form the cookies, about 1 rounded tablespoon each, and place on the prepared cookie sheets, leaving 2 inches between them to allow for spreading. Press the center of each cookie with your thumb to make an indentation, then fill each one with 1 teaspoon of the jam.

Bake the cookies one pan at a time for 10 to 12 minutes, rotating the pan halfway through the baking, until they are golden on the edges and the jam is bubbling. Let cool completely on a wire rack.

The cookies can be stored in an airtight container at room temperature for up to 4 days.

CHOCOLATE CREAM SAMMIES

Makes 12 sandwich cookies

Everyone loves Oreos, but this homemade version is so much better. The wafer cookies have a deep, rich chocolate flavor, and when sandwiched with the sweet vanilla filling, they create a heavenly experience. I also like to stuff the cookies with fresh strawberry ice cream to make mini ice cream sandwiches, but any ice cream will work.

1⅓ cups unbleached all-purpose flour
1 cup Dutch-processed cocoa powder, sifted
2¼ teaspoons baking soda
¼ teaspoon fine sea salt

½ pound (2 sticks) unsalted butter, at room temperature
1 cup granulated sugar
½ cup packed light brown sugar
2 large eggs

FOR THE FILLING

8 tablespoons (1 stick) unsalted butter, at room temperature
4 cups confectioners' sugar
¼ cup whole milk
1 teaspoon pure vanilla extract

Line two cookie sheets with parchment.

In a medium bowl, whisk together the flour, cocoa powder, baking soda, and salt. Set aside.

In the bowl of a stand mixer fitted with the paddle attachment (or in a large mixing bowl, using a handheld mixer), cream together the butter and both sugars on medium-high speed for 3 to 5 minutes, until light and fluffy. Scrape down the bottom and sides of the bowl. Turn the mixer speed down to low and add the eggs one at a time, mixing well after each addition and scraping down the sides of the bowl with a rubber spatula as necessary.

With the mixer on low speed, add the dry ingredients, beating until just combined.

Remove the bowl from the mixer and finish mixing by hand to make sure no bits of flour or butter are hiding on the bottom of the bowl and the dough is thoroughly mixed. Cover the bowl with plastic wrap and chill in the refrigerator until the dough is firm, about 30 minutes.

Position the racks in the middle and lower third of the oven and preheat the oven to 350°F.

Use a small ice cream scoop to form the cookies, about 1 rounded tablespoon each, and place on the prepared cookie sheets, leaving 2 inches between them to allow for spreading.

continued

Bake the cookies for 8 to 10 minutes, rotating the pans halfway through baking, until they are slightly cracked and firm in the center and the smell of chocolate has begun to fill the kitchen. Transfer the cookies to a wire rack to cool completely.

To make the filling: In the bowl of a stand mixer fitted with the paddle attachment (or in a large mixing bowl, using a handheld mixer), cream the butter on medium speed for 2 to 3 minutes, until light and fluffy. Add 2 cups of the confectioners' sugar, about half of the milk, and the vanilla and mix on low speed for 1 to 2 minutes, until smooth and creamy. Add the remaining milk and mix until incorporated, 1 to 2 minutes. Gradually add the remaining confectioners' sugar, mixing until the filling is light and fluffy, 2 to 3 minutes.

The filling can be stored in an airtight container at room temperature for up to 2 days or refrigerated for up to 1 week. To use filling that has been chilled, remove from the refrigerator and bring to room temperature; make sure that it is softened before you use it. Transfer the filling to a stand mixer fitted with the paddle attachment (or use a handheld mixer) and beat on medium-high speed until light and fluffy, 2 to 3 minutes.

To assemble the cookies: Put about 1 tablespoon of filling on the bottom of one cookie, place another cookie right side up on top, and press gently together. Repeat with the remaining cookies.

The cookies can be stored in an airtight container at room temperature for up to 5 days.

MARSHMALLOW–CHOCOLATE COOKIE SAMMIES

This is our version of a favorite Southern confection called the moon pie. The graham cracker cookies are sandwiched around a gooey marshmallow filling and dunked in a rich chocolate coating.

Makes about 12 sandwich cookies

3 cups unbleached all-purpose flour

2½ cups fine graham cracker crumbs

1½ teaspoons fine sea salt

1 teaspoon baking powder, preferably aluminum-free

1 teaspoon baking soda

¾ teaspoon ground cinnamon

¾ pound (3 sticks) unsalted butter, at room temperature

½ cup packed light brown sugar

½ cup sorghum

½ teaspoon pure vanilla extract

¼ cup whole milk

FOR THE MARSHMALLOW FILLING

¾ cup granulated sugar

6 tablespoons water

¼ cup light corn syrup

1 tablespoon honey

Pinch of fine sea salt

1 envelope unflavored gelatin

1 teaspoon pure vanilla extract

FOR THE CHOCOLATE COATING

2 pounds semisweet chocolate chips

½ cup vegetable oil

SPECIAL EQUIPMENT

One 3-inch round cookie cutter

Candy thermometer

In a large mixing bowl, whisk together the flour, graham cracker crumbs, salt, baking powder, baking soda, and cinnamon. Set aside.

In the bowl of a stand mixer fitted with the paddle attachment (or in a large mixing bowl, using a handheld mixer), cream together the butter, brown sugar, sorghum, and vanilla on medium speed for 3 to 5 minutes, until light and fluffy.

Turn the speed down to low and gradually add the flour and graham cracker mixture, beating until just combined; scrape down the bottom and sides of the bowl as necessary. Add the milk and mix just until incorporated.

continued

Divide the dough in half and put one half on a sheet of parchment. Place a piece of plastic wrap on top of the dough and use a rolling pin to roll it out to about ½ inch thick. Remove the plastic wrap and slide the dough, on the parchment, onto a cookie sheet. Repeat with the remaining dough. Cover with plastic wrap and chill in the refrigerator for at least 30 minutes, or up to 2 weeks.

Position the racks in the middle and lower third of the oven and preheat the oven to 325°F.

Remove one cookie sheet of dough from the refrigerator and transfer the cookie dough, on the parchment, to the kitchen counter. Cut out cookies with a 3-inch round cookie cutter. Line the cookie sheet with fresh parchment and place the cookies on the pan, leaving about 1 inch between them. Chill the cookies in the refrigerator for at least 15 minutes while you cut out the second sheet of cookies. You can use the scraps of dough one time to cut out more cookies.

Bake the cookies for 10 to 12 minutes, rotating the pans halfway through baking, until they are firm to the touch and lightly golden. Let cool completely on wire racks.

To make the filling: In a large saucepan, combine the sugar, 3 tablespoons of the water, the corn syrup, honey, and salt and stir over medium heat until the sugar is dissolved. Clip a candy thermometer to the side of the pan and, without stirring, bring to a boil, then cook until the syrup reaches 240°F, about 10 minutes.

Meanwhile, pour the remaining 3 tablespoons of water into the bowl of a stand mixer fitted with the whisk attachment (or use a large mixing bowl and a handheld mixer), sprinkle the gelatin over the top, and mix on low speed until the gelatin softens.

With the mixer on low speed, gradually pour the hot sugar syrup into the gelatin mixture, then beat, gradually increasing the speed to high, for 10 to 12 minutes, until the mixture holds stiff peaks. Turn the speed down to low, add the vanilla, and mix to incorporate.

To assemble the cookies: Fill a pastry bag (or a ziplock bag) fitted with a plain tip with the filling (cut off one bottom corner if using a plastic bag) and pipe about 2 heaping tablespoons of marshmallow filling onto the bottom of one cookie. Place another cookie right side up on top and gently press down to seal. Repeat with the remaining cookies and filling.

To coat the cookies: Set a heatproof bowl over a pan of simmering water (make sure the bottom of the bowl does not touch the water), add the chocolate chips and oil, and stir frequently until the chips have completely melted. Remove the bowl from the heat.

Set a wire rack on a cookie sheet lined with wax paper or parchment to catch the chocolate drips. Using two forks, dunk each cookie sandwich into the warm chocolate, turning to coat, and gently place the cookie on the wire rack. If the chocolate begins to harden, return it to the simmering water and stir until smooth again. Let the cookies sit until set.

The cookies can be stored in an airtight container at room temperature for up to 3 days.

DECORATED SUGAR COOKIES

Sugar cookies are pure fun to eat, and with a few tips, decorating them can be even more fun. See pages 248–249 for my tricks for making sugar cookies that your kids will love!

Makes 24 to 36 cookies, depending on the size of the cutter(s)

3 cups unbleached all-purpose flour
¾ teaspoon fine sea salt
½ teaspoon baking powder, preferably aluminum-free

10 ounces (2½ sticks) unsalted butter, at room temperature
1 cup granulated sugar
1 large egg
1 large egg yolk
1 teaspoon pure vanilla extract

Royal Icing (see How to Decorate Sugar Cookies, page 248)

SPECIAL EQUIPMENT
One 3- to 4-inch cookie cutter (any shape you like)

In a medium bowl, whisk together the flour, salt, and baking powder. Set aside.

In the bowl of a stand mixer fitted with the paddle attachment (or in a large mixing bowl, using a handheld mixer), cream together the butter and sugar on medium speed for 1 to 2 minutes, until light and creamy. Add the egg, egg yolk, and vanilla and beat for 3 to 5 minutes, until light and fluffy.

Add the dry ingredients in thirds, beating until just combined.

Remove the bowl from the mixer and finish mixing by hand to make sure no bits of flour or butter are hiding on the bottom of the bowl and the dough is thoroughly mixed.

Divide the dough in half, shape each piece into a disk, and wrap each one in plastic. Put the disks in the refrigerator to chill for at least 2 hours, or overnight (the dough can also be frozen, tightly wrapped, for up to 1 month).

When ready to make the cookies, remove one of the disks of dough from the refrigerator and let sit at room temperature until it is softened enough to roll out but still quite firm (it will continue to soften as you work with it).

Line two cookie sheets with parchment. Transfer the softened dough to a lightly floured surface. Place a piece of plastic wrap or wax paper on top and, using a rolling pin, roll out the dough to a ¼-inch thickness. Using a 3- to 4-inch cookie cutter, cut out cookies and place about 2 inches apart on the prepared cookie sheets. Put the cookies in the refrigerator to chill for at least 30 minutes before baking. (Once you've baked the first batch, repeat with the remaining dough. You can reroll the scraps and cut out more cookies just one time.)

Position the racks in the middle and lower third of the oven and preheat the oven to 325°F.

Bake the cookies for 10 to 12 minutes, rotating the pans halfway through the baking time, until the edges are lightly golden. Let completely cool on wire racks. Undecorated cookies can be frozen in an airtight container for up to 2 weeks.

Follow the instructions on pages 248–249 to decorate the sugar cookies (or simply enjoy the cookies plain). Store cookies in an airtight container for up to 1 week.

HOW TO DECORATE SUGAR COOKIES

Royal icing is the base for decorating sugar cookies. I like to use meringue powder instead of egg whites in the icing because it is safe to eat even for small children. Royal icing dries with a hard, smooth, matte finish, giving you the perfect canvas to paint on.

To make royal icing, you will need one 1-pound box confectioners' sugar, 5 tablespoons meringue powder (see Resources, page 293), and about ½ cup water; mix together in a medium bowl. You'll use this icing at various times to decorate the cookies; keep it covered with plastic wrap when it's not in use to prevent a crust from forming on the surface. However, if it gets too stiff, you can always add a few drops of water to thin it out.

Scoop some of the icing into a pastry bag fitted with a #3 small round tip. Pipe a thin border of royal icing just inside the cookie's edge. You will want the icing to be stiff like meringue to pipe the border. Let the icing dry completely before filling in the surface of the cookie.

Once the border has set, add a little water to thin the icing just a bit so that it will be looser and spread easier as you fill in the surface of the cookie. Then scoop the icing into another pastry bag fitted with a #4 tip. Starting from the top of the cookie, fill the cookie with the icing, using a zigzag motion. Gently shake the cookie from side to side to settle any air bubbles, leaving a smooth surface. Let the icing set until firm and dry, at least 2 hours.

To paint the cookies, you will need luster dust (see Resources, page 293) or food coloring and a few drops of lemon extract. In a small bowl, combine your royal icing with about 1 teaspoon luster dust or powdered food coloring and a few drops of lemon extract, adding more extract as needed until the mixture is the consistency of thin paint. Repeat this process for each color icing you want to create.

You can use a pastry bag fitted with a #3 or a #4 small round tip, a Q-tip, or a small paintbrush to decorate the cookies. Paint designs onto the iced cookies, blotting the Q-tip or brush on a paper towel as needed. Let dry at room temperature, uncovered, on a baking sheet for at least 2 hours or overnight, depending on the humidity in your area. If you are packaging the cookies for party favors, be sure to plan in advance and let them dry overnight. Never, ever refrigerate the cookies. Carefully place them in an airtight container for up to 2 weeks.

COOKIE DECORATING STEP-BY-STEP

Using a pastry bag fitted with a small plain tip, pipe a thin border of royal icing just inside the cookie's edge. Let the border dry completely.

Add a little water to thin the icing, and then fill in the cookie using a zigzag motion with a #4 plain round tip. Let dry, at least 2 hours.

This is when you can be creative with your decorations.

Use a Q-tip or a small paintbrush to paint designs onto the icing. Blot the Q-tip or brush on a paper towel as needed.

Use a different cotton swab or brush for each color.

Let the cookies dry and enjoy!

PB&J SAMMIES

This peanut butter and jelly sammie is like the good old-fashioned lunchtime favorite. It's double the goodness; be sure to use your favorite jam.

Makes 12 sandwich cookies

1½ cups unbleached all-purpose flour
1 teaspoon baking soda
¼ teaspoon fine sea salt
8 tablespoons (1 stick) unsalted butter, at room temperature

½ cup granulated sugar
½ cup packed light brown sugar
½ cup creamy peanut butter
1 large egg

½ teaspoon pure vanilla extract
¾ cup jam (your favorite flavor)

Position the racks in the middle and lower third of the oven and preheat the oven to 375°F. Line two cookie sheets with parchment.

In a large mixing bowl, whisk together the flour, baking soda, and salt. Set aside.

In the bowl of a stand mixer fitted with the paddle attachment (or in a large mixing bowl, using a handheld mixer), cream together the butter, both sugars, and peanut butter on medium speed for 3 to 5 minutes, until light and fluffy. Add the egg and vanilla and beat for 1 to 2 minutes, until fluffy.

Add the dry ingredients in thirds, beating until just combined. Finish mixing by hand.

Use a small ice cream scoop to form the cookies, about 1 rounded tablespoon each, and place on the prepared cookie sheets, leaving 2 inches between them to allow for spreading. Flatten the tops with the palm of your hand and then use the tines of a fork to create a crisscross pattern on the top.

Bake the cookies for 10 to 12 minutes, rotating the pans halfway through the baking time, until they are golden brown. Let cool completely on a wire rack.

To make the sammies: Put a dollop of jam (about 1 tablespoon) on the bottom of one of the cookies, place another cookie right side up on top, and press together gently. Repeat with the remaining cookies and jam.

The cookies can be stored in an airtight container at room temperature for up to 3 days.

COTTON CANDY MERINGUES

These sweet confections are light and airy, with a delightful chewy texture. Made with egg whites and sugar, and without flour, they are the perfect treats for gluten-free friends. I like to tint these cookies in pastel shades to match our cupcakes.

Makes 12 meringues

4 large egg whites, at room temperature
¼ teaspoon cream of tartar
1 cup granulated sugar
2 teaspoons cornstarch

1 teaspoon white wine vinegar
1½ teaspoons pure vanilla extract

Liquid gel food coloring (optional)

SPECIAL EQUIPMENT
One 3-inch round cookie cutter

Position a rack in the lower third of the oven and preheat the oven to 250°F. Line a baking sheet with parchment. Using a 3-inch round cookie cutter as a guide, trace 12 circles at least 1 inch apart on the parchment, then turn the parchment over to use these circles as your guide.

In the bowl of a stand mixer fitted with the whisk attachment (or in a large mixing bowl, using a handheld mixer), whip the egg whites and cream of tartar on high speed until the whites form soft peaks. Gradually add the sugar and cornstarch, then whip until the meringue forms stiff, shiny peaks.

Remove the bowl from the mixer and gently fold in the vinegar and vanilla. Fold in a few drops of food coloring, if using.

Using a large spoon, gently scoop mounds of meringue, about 2 inches high, into the traced circles on the prepared baking sheet. Smooth the sides with a butter knife.

Bake the meringues for 1¼ to 1½ hours, until they are set to the touch. Turn the oven off and let the meringues cool in the oven for 1½ hours.

The meringues can be stored in an airtight container at room temperature for up to 5 days.

STAR BROWNIES

Makes 16 brownies

These rich, melt-in-your-mouth chocolate brownies have been a favorite at the bakery from day one. Back in the day, we hand-mixed the batter, and I always had to count the strokes to make sure it was properly mixed. These days, we make the batter in a stand mixer, but here I give you the counting-strokes method. It's a little tedious, but it's the most reliable method I know, and it makes for a fantastic brownie.

½ pound (2 sticks) unsalted butter, cut into cubes
½ pound unsweetened chocolate, preferably Scharffen Berger 99%, chopped

2½ cups granulated sugar
1½ teaspoons fine sea salt
1 tablespoon pure vanilla extract
4 large eggs, at room temperature

1 cup unbleached all-purpose flour

Confectioners' sugar for dusting (optional)

Position a rack in the lower third of the oven and preheat the oven to 350°F. Lightly spray a 9-by-9-inch baking pan with nonstick spray. Line with parchment, leaving an overhang on two opposite sides of the pan.

Set a medium heatproof bowl over a saucepan of simmering water (make sure the bowl does not touch the water), add the cubed butter and chocolate, and stir frequently until melted and smooth.

Remove the bowl from the heat, add the sugar, salt, and vanilla, and stir with a wooden spoon until thoroughly combined. Add one egg and beat it in, counting 100 strokes. Add the remaining eggs one at a time, counting 100 strokes after each one. It's an arm workout, but it wasn't so bad, right?

Add the flour and fold it into the batter until just combined.

Pour the batter into the prepared baking pan. Bake for 50 to 55 minutes, until a slight crack has formed around the edges. Place the pan on a wire rack and let the brownies cool completely.

Using the parchment "handles," remove the brownies from the pan. Remove the parchment and cut the brownies into 16 squares. You can decorate the top with confectioners' sugar, if you'd like. I use a stencil of a star, of course.

The brownies can be stored in an airtight container at room temperature for up to 5 days.

I like to refrigerate the brownies, which makes them extra chewy and fudgy—yum.

SHAKER MEYER LEMON PIE BARS

Makes 12 bars

The Shakers wasted nothing, and they used whole lemons in this pie bar. That's right—rind, pith, and all go into the filling. Be sure to slice the lemons as thin as you can and let them macerate in sugar for at least 3 hours (the longer, the better). The result is a tart lemony filling similar in texture to marmalade. You can substitute regular lemons, if Meyer lemons are not in season.

FOR THE FILLING

2 large Meyer lemons, scrubbed
2 cups granulated sugar
4 large eggs
¼ teaspoon fine sea salt

FOR THE CRUST

½ pound (2 sticks) unsalted butter, melted
½ cup granulated sugar
1½ teaspoons pure vanilla extract
1½ teaspoons fine sea salt
2 cups unbleached all-purpose flour

SPECIAL EQUIPMENT

Mandoline or other vegetable slicer

To prepare the lemons for the filling: Slice the stem ends off the lemons. Using a mandoline, slice the lemons paper-thin and place them in a nonreactive bowl, like glass or stainless steel (do not use aluminum). Pick out and discard all the seeds. Add the sugar to the lemons and toss together with your hands. Cover the bowl with plastic wrap and let sit at room temperature for at least 3 hours, or up to 12 hours. The skin of the lemons will soften and the sugar will completely dissolve. If you see any seeds floating on top, discard them.

Position a rack in the middle of the oven and preheat the oven to 350°F. Line a 9-by-9-by-2-inch baking pan with parchment, letting the ends of the parchment hang over two opposite sides of the pan.

To make the crust: In a medium bowl, stir together the butter, sugar, vanilla, and salt until well blended. Add the flour in thirds and stir until just incorporated.

Press the mixture evenly into the bottom of the prepared pan. Prick the crust all over with a fork. Bake for 15 to 18 minutes, until the crust is golden. Set aside to cool while you make the filling. (Leave the oven on.)

To make the filling: In a small bowl, whisk the eggs and salt together. Add to the lemon mixture and stir to combine.

Pour the filling into the prebaked crust. Bake for 30 to 40 minutes, until golden and the center no longer jiggles. Place on a wire rack to cool, then refrigerate before cutting and serving.

The bars can be stored in an airtight container in the refrigerator for up to 3 days.

SALTED CARAMEL POPCORN

Warning: this stuff is addictive! Back up, Jack—homemade caramel-coated popcorn is so much better than anything out of a box. You can hide a fun prize at the bottom of each serving if you like.

*Makes about
10 cups*

10 cups popped corn (about ⅓ cup unpopped kernels)
1 cup packed light brown sugar
¼ cup light corn syrup
2 tablespoons water

6 tablespoons unsalted butter
¼ teaspoon fine sea salt
1 tablespoon pure vanilla extract
½ teaspoon baking soda
1½ cups whole almonds

1 teaspoon flaky sea salt, such as Jacobsen or Maldon

SPECIAL EQUIPMENT
Candy thermometer

Preheat the oven to 250°F. Line a baking sheet with parchment.

Butter a very large bowl. Pour in the popped popcorn.

In a medium heavy saucepan, combine the brown sugar, corn syrup, water, butter, and fine sea salt and give it all a good stir, then cook over medium heat, stirring, until the sugar has dissolved and the butter is completely melted. Clip a candy thermometer to the side of the pan and cook until the mixture reaches 250°F, about 5 minutes.

Remove the pan from the heat and quickly but carefully whisk in the vanilla and baking soda. The mixture will bubble and foam and start to lighten in color.

Pour all of the caramel goo over the popcorn, using a heatproof spatula to make sure that it is all coated as evenly as possible. Stir in the almonds.

Spread the caramelized popcorn on the prepared baking sheet in a single layer. Bake for 45 minutes to 1 hour, tossing it every 15 minutes or so and checking for color toward the end of baking, until the popcorn is golden brown and smells delicious. Sprinkle with the flaky sea salt. Set aside to cool completely or eat it warm!

The popcorn can be stored at room temperature in an airtight container for up to 3 days.

LEMON BUTTERMILK FUDGE

Makes 16 pieces

My grandma Hannah loved fudge and usually made the chocolate-nutty kind, but on occasion, she would use the last bit of buttermilk in the jug to make buttermilk fudge. I like to add a bit of lemon zest to complement the sweet tanginess of buttermilk.

½ cup pecan pieces
2 cups granulated sugar
1 cup buttermilk
8 tablespoons (1 stick) unsalted butter, cut into cubes

1 tablespoon honey
⅛ teaspoon fine sea salt
Grated zest of 1 lemon
Flaky sea salt, such as Jacobsen or Maldon, for sprinkling (optional)

SPECIAL EQUIPMENT
Candy thermometer

Preheat the oven to 350°F. Line an 8-by-8-by-2-inch pan with parchment, leaving an overhang on two opposite sides of the pan.

Spread the pecans in a pie pan and toast in the oven for about 5 minutes, until fragrant. Set aside and turn off the oven.

In a medium saucepan, combine the sugar, buttermilk, butter, honey, and fine sea salt and cook over medium-high heat, stirring occasionally, until the butter has melted and the sugar has dissolved. When the mixture comes to a boil, brush the sides of the saucepan with a pastry brush dipped in water, to remove any sugar crystals; do not stir again. Reduce the heat, clip a candy thermometer to the side of the pan, and simmer, without stirring, until the thermometer reaches 238°F (this is the "soft ball stage"), 10 to 15 minutes. The fudge will be pale golden and smell of toffee.

Pour the mixture into the bowl of a stand mixer fitted with the paddle attachment (or use a medium mixing bowl and a handheld mixer). Turn the mixer on to medium-high speed and beat, scraping down the sides of the bowl, until the fudge is thickened, stiff, and matte, 5 to 8 minutes.

Add the toasted pecans and lemon zest and mix until combined. The fudge may break up when you add these ingredients, but continue to mix, and it will become smooth again.

Transfer the fudge to the prepared pan and use an offset spatula to smooth the top. Sprinkle with flakes of sea salt, if desired. Let set for at least an hour, then remove from the pan, and cut into squares.

The fudge can be stored in an airtight container at room temperature for up to 1 week.

CUPCAKE SURPRISE BALL

As a child, I would plead my case for anything that had a surprise inside, from breakfast cereal to Cracker Jacks. Christmas stocking surprises are still my absolute favorite. I am a bit of a magpie when it comes to collecting small treasures. I "hunt and gather" vintage trinkets wherever I go. So I love making these little paper balls and filling them with tiny treats. You can fill them with all sorts of goodies, like stickers, cupcake toppers, and old-fashioned hard candy. You can find a treasure trove of goodies in your local party store or on Etsy. Think of these as mini piñatas or a surprise party in a ball, and make them as favors for your next celebration. *Makes 1 surprise ball*

MATERIALS

Prizes, such as a variety of hard candy,
tiny toys, and stickers (10 to 15 per ball)
Crepe paper streamers, in one color or
assorted colors
Confetti
White glue, such as Elmer's
Clear glitter
Cupcake liners
Large (1-inch) red beads

TOOLS

Paintbrush
Scissors

Step 1: Start with the largest prize you want to include in the ball. I like to use a round object, such as a small rubber ball, as a starting point. Wrap the first treasure in a crepe paper streamer, tightly but not so tight that the paper rips, until it is completely covered. Then add the next treasure to the bundle and continue to wrap, using one continuous strip of crepe paper. Add confetti between the layers of prizes for another surprise. Repeat until all of your prizes are wrapped up in a ball. Use dabs of glue as needed to keep the crepe paper strands from unraveling, and to keep a round shape, roll the ball in your hands as you would a ball of dough.

Step 2: Using a paintbrush, lightly coat the entire ball with glue and then roll in clear glitter, to create the appearance of a sugarcoated treat. Allow to dry.

Step 3: Stack two cupcake liners, with glue in between for added support. Let dry.

Step 4: Put a bead of glue in the bottom of the stacked liners and attach the glitter-coated ball. Let dry, then add a bead of glue around the seam of the ball and liner and roll it in multicolored confetti.

Step 5: Put a cherry on top! Glue the red bead to the top of your surprise ball, and you've made the sweetest party favor of all time.

MAKE IT FOR A RAINY DAY

JAMS, SPREADS, AND MAKE-AHEAD TREATS

One cold, rainy Monday, our favorite farmers, Cat and Bradley, invited us to spend the day on their beautiful sprawling farm a couple of hours down the road, in Sylvania, Georgia. Griff and I love road trips, so we packed up some biscuits, jam, and a pie and headed out of town. As soon as we turned onto Buttermilk Road, I knew it was going to be a day of good food and fellowship.

Bradley founded L. J. Woods Farm as an experiment in family farming, sustainable livestock practices, and the conservation of Southern heritage breeds. It has grown to become a great source for some of the best restaurants in the South. And farm living was made for me . . . well, at least for that one day. I filled huge baskets with all sorts of eggs, including duck eggs and my favorite Ameraucana chicken eggs. We visited Bradley's prized Ossabaw Island hogs and checked out the Pineywoods cattle, and I held one of the baby Spanish goats. And when Cat and Bradley sent us home with jars of pickled vegetables and wild watermelon rind that we had sampled throughout the day, Griff and I were both feeling inspired.

A day on a real working farm got me to thinking about what I could preserve on my own. My grandma Hannah would have "putting up" days, which she said were a celebration of the season's harvest. Now I like to spend entire Sundays making jam with summer berries; I love knowing that I can reach into the pantry for a jar of Blackberry Lime Jam (page 269) in the middle of winter to brighten my day. It's a great reminder too that the seasons will change once again, and before you know it, you will have a big ol' pot of Apple Butter (page 274) on the stove (or use a slow cooker, as I do!) from delicious apples you picked yourself. The simple recipes in this chapter are for "refrigerator preserves"; no need for sterilizing jars and canning in a water bath.

There is nothing that you can buy on the grocery shelves today that will be as flavorful as something you made from scratch, and you will be amazed at how simple it is to make your own condiments at home. At the bakery, folks are delighted by the care we take to make everything from our Homemade Syrups (page 286) to Lemon Butter Bean Spread (page 278). It's an affordable, delicious, and creative outlet to make all sorts of foods yourself that you can enjoy for weeks to come.

RASPBERRY JAM

Makes 2 pints

Making homemade jam is easier than you might think, and it requires only two ingredients: fruit and sugar. This seedless jam is great poured over baked Brie or even spread between the layers of a cake, but be sure to try it in our Jam Muffins (page 15) or with the Old-Fashioned Buttermilk Biscuits (page 35).

2¼ pounds raspberries
3 cups granulated sugar

SPECIAL EQUIPMENT
Candy thermometer

Medium-mesh strainer
Mason jars (optional)

Put a saucer in the freezer, along with three metal spoons.

Rinse the raspberries in a colander under cold running water and drain. Put the berries in a large heavy nonreactive saucepan and toss them with the sugar. Cook over medium-low heat, stirring and mashing the berries with a heatproof spatula, until the sugar is dissolved and the berries have released a lot of juice, about 10 minutes. Clip a candy thermometer to the pan, gradually raise the heat to high, stirring frequently, and then continue to cook, stirring constantly and scraping the bottom of the pan so the mixture does not stick (if it does begin to stick, turn down the heat just a bit), until the jam registers 220°F on the candy thermometer, 15 to 20 minutes after it reaches a rolling boil. The jam will look glossy and dark. To check for doneness, put a teaspoon of the jam on the cold plate and return the plate to the freezer for 3 to 4 minutes. If you can make a line through the jam with your finger that doesn't disappear, it's ready. If the jam is still too runny, continue to cook and test until ready.

Immediately transfer the jam to a medium-mesh strainer set over a heatproof mixing bowl and force the jam through the strainer; discard the seeds. Carefully skim any foam from the top with a spoon. Let cool.

Store the jam in Mason jars or in an airtight container in the refrigerator for up to 2 weeks.

BLACKBERRY LIME JAM

Makes 2 pints

Blackberries have a sweet tartness that comes alive when you use them to make jam. We add lime, which gives the beautiful purple jam a zest of citrusy sunshine and brightens the flavor of the blackberries. This jam begs to be put on your morning toast.

3½ pounds blackberries
1¾ cups granulated sugar

Grated zest of 2 limes
¼ cup fresh lime juice

SPECIAL EQUIPMENT
Candy thermometer
Mason jars (optional)

Put a saucer in the freezer, along with three metal spoons.

Rinse the blackberries in a colander under cold running water and drain. Put the berries in a large heavy nonreactive saucepan and toss them with the sugar, lime zest, and lime juice. Cook over low heat, stirring, until the sugar has dissolved and the berries have released a lot of juice, about 10 minutes. Clip a candy thermometer to the pan, gradually raise the heat to high, stirring frequently, and then continue to cook, stirring constantly and scraping the bottom of the pan so the mixture does not stick (if the mixture does begin to stick, turn down the heat slightly), until the jam registers 220°F on the candy thermometer, 15 to 20 minutes after it reaches a rolling boil. The jam will look glossy and dark. To check for doneness, put a teaspoon of the jam on the cold plate and return the plate to the freezer for 3 to 4 minutes. If you can make a line through the jam with your finger that doesn't disappear, it's ready. If the jam is still too runny, continue to cook and test until ready.

Immediately transfer the jam to a medium-mesh strainer set over a heatproof mixing bowl and force the jam through the strainer; discard the seeds. Carefully skim any foam from the top with a spoon. Let cool.

Store the jam in Mason jars or in an airtight container in the refrigerator for up to 2 weeks.

GREEN TOMATO MARMALADE

Makes about 2 quarts

When we grow tomatoes in our backyard, we usually pick a bunch early in the season to make this yummy marmalade. As the tomatoes cook down with the ginger and lemon into a spicy marmalade, we can't wait for it to cool to sample some. Spoon it over cream cheese and serve with crackers for an easy snack.

4 pounds green tomatoes, finely chopped

¼ cup finely minced peeled fresh ginger

Grated zest and juice of 1 large lemon

1 teaspoon red pepper flakes (optional)

5 cups granulated sugar

OPTIONAL SPECIAL EQUIPMENT

Mason jars

In a large ceramic bowl, combine the green tomatoes, ginger, lemon zest, juice, and red pepper flakes, if using, and stir to mix. Add the sugar and stir well. Cover with plastic wrap and refrigerate overnight, 12 to 24 hours.

Transfer the tomato mixture to a large nonreactive pot and bring to a boil over medium-high heat. Reduce the heat to medium-low and simmer, stirring occasionally, until the mixture thickens, about 1 hour. Remove from the heat and let cool.

Store the marmalade in Mason jars or in an airtight container in the refrigerator for up to 2 weeks.

VIDALIA ONION MARMALADE

*Makes about
2½ cups*

As strange as it may sound, one of my favorite vegetables is the onion, because of its subtle sweetness. The complex flavors of raw onions hit you right away: bitter, sharp, sour—but when you cook them, the natural sugars come to life. We love to use onion marmalade on hamburgers, pizza, or grilled sandwiches. It's a great condiment to make ahead and store in your fridge for when you crave it.

3 tablespoons olive oil

2 tablespoons unsalted butter

6 cups thinly sliced Vidalia onions (about 3 pounds)

1 cup packed light brown sugar

¾ cup cider vinegar

2 tablespoons balsamic vinegar

1 tablespoon grated peeled fresh ginger

½ teaspoon red pepper flakes

½ teaspoon dried thyme

½ cup golden raisins, chopped

OPTIONAL SPECIAL EQUIPMENT

Mason jars

In a large heavy saucepan, combine the olive oil, butter, and onions and cook over medium-high heat until the onions are translucent and beginning to brown on the edges, 10 to 15 minutes.

Add the brown sugar, both vinegars, the ginger, red pepper flakes, thyme, and raisins and stir to combine. Bring to a simmer, then reduce the heat to medium and simmer until the onions are a deep golden color and the liquid has reduced to a syrupy consistency, 30 to 40 minutes. Remove from the heat and let cool; as the marmalade cools, the syrup will thicken.

Store in Mason jars or an airtight container in the refrigerator for up to 2 weeks.

SWEET POTATO COMEBACK SAUCE

Makes about 2 cups

While traveling through Mississippi on our first book tour, we tasted something called "comeback sauce," a mayonnaise-based condiment that's a little sweet and a little spicy. Griff knew he had to make his own version when we got home, and he came up with this recipe. It's a versatile condiment that has lots of tasty uses—try it as a dipping sauce for French fries or hush puppies, or as a topping for fried fish. One of our favorite ways to enjoy it is in our Thanksgiving sandwich (see page 144).

1 large sweet potato
⅓ cup mayonnaise
1 tablespoon olive oil
1 tablespoon fresh lemon juice

1 large garlic clove, finely chopped
¾ teaspoon ground ginger
¾ teaspoon smoked paprika
½ teaspoon ground cumin

½ teaspoon cayenne pepper
½ teaspoon fine sea salt
½ teaspoon freshly ground black pepper

Position a rack in the middle of the oven and preheat the oven to 400°F.

Wrap the sweet potato in aluminum foil. Bake for 45 to 60 minutes, until tender. Let cool completely, then split open and scrape out the flesh.

In the bowl of a food processor, combine the sweet potato, mayonnaise, olive oil, lemon juice, garlic, ginger, paprika, cumin, cayenne, salt, and pepper and process until smooth. Transfer to an airtight container, cover, and refrigerate for at least 4 hours before using.

The sauce can be refrigerated for up to 1 week.

APPLE BUTTER

*Makes
2 pints*

Apple butter is best when cooked low and slow, and so the best equipment for the job is a slow cooker. Get it started in the morning, and the next morning, you'll be slathering it on biscuits, stirring some into your yogurt and Good-Morning Granola (page 46), or spreading it on buttered toast.

3 pounds Fuji, Honeycrisp, or Gala apples, peeled, cored, and cut into 1-inch chunks
4 cups water
1 cup apple cider

¾ cup granulated sugar
¼ teaspoon ground cinnamon
¼ teaspoon ground cloves
¼ teaspoon ground cardamom

¼ teaspoon ground allspice

SPECIAL EQUIPMENT
4- to 6-quart slow cooker
Mason jars (optional)

Put the apples into a large heavy pot, add the water, cider, and sugar, and bring to a boil over high heat. Continue to boil, stirring occasionally, until the apples are completely broken down, 30 to 40 minutes. Remove from the heat.

Puree the apples in batches in a food processor or blender. Add the cinnamon, cloves, cardamom, and allspice and stir to combine. Pour the puree into a 4- to 6-quart slow cooker and cook on the low setting, with the lid propped slightly open, for 9 to 12 hours, until thick and dark. Use an immersion blender to blitz the puree a few times during the process, to make sure the consistency is as smooth as butter. (Or puree the finished apple butter in a food processor, in batches if necessary.) Let cool.

Store the apple butter in Mason jars or in an airtight container in the refrigerator for up to 2 weeks.

ICEBOX PICKLES

Makes 6 cups

There's no hiding the fact that we are hooked on pickles—we love sweet pickles, spicy pickles, sour pickles . . . you name it. It's a good thing we like to make them as much as we like to eat them. Our version of icebox pickles is a quick pickle that is a good introduction to get you into pickling too.

1⅓ cups distilled white vinegar
1⅓ cups water
4 teaspoons granulated sugar

2 teaspoons fine sea salt
1 pound English cucumbers, sliced ¼ inch thick
1 small sweet onion, thinly sliced

2 large garlic cloves, crushed and peeled
1 tablespoon pickling spice
¼ teaspoon red pepper flakes

In a quart jar or other container with a lid, combine the vinegar, water, sugar, and salt and stir to dissolve the sugar and salt.

Add the cucumbers, onion, garlic, pickling spice, and red pepper flakes and stir well; make sure the cucumbers are submerged. Cover tightly and refrigerate for 24 to 48 hours before digging in.

Store the pickles in the refrigerator for up to 2 weeks.

PICKLED RED ONIONS

Makes about 3 cups

Quick-pickling is easy to do; you get immediate satisfaction, and you don't have to go through the whole process of canning. We keep these pickled onions in our fridge all the time. The blend of spices and the crunch of the onions make them delicious in salads, and on hot dogs and hamburgers too.

2 pounds red onions, thinly sliced

1 tablespoon red pepper flakes

1 tablespoon pickling spice

1 teaspoon fine sea salt

¼ teaspoon anise seeds

1 bay leaf

2 cups distilled white vinegar

2 cups granulated sugar

Combine the onions, red pepper flakes, pickling spice, salt, anise seeds, and bay leaf in a large heatproof bowl. Set aside.

In a large nonreactive saucepan, combine the vinegar and sugar and bring to a boil over medium-high heat, stirring to dissolve the sugar. Remove from the heat and pour over the onions, stirring the onions and spices with the liquid. Make sure the onions are submerged in the liquid and let cool to room temperature.

You can eat the onions immediately, but they are better after a day or two. They can be stored in an airtight container in the refrigerator for up to 2 weeks.

LEMON BUTTER BEAN SPREAD

Serve this bean spread, which has the consistency of hummus, as a dip or a spread to accompany a vegetable tray with crackers, or use as a spread on a vegetarian sandwich filled with crunchy vegetables.

Makes about 4 cups

4 cups cooked butter beans
½ cup fresh lemon juice
1½ teaspoons ground
  cumin

1½ teaspoons freshly
  ground black pepper
2 large garlic cloves, finely
  chopped

⅓ cup olive oil

Combine the butter beans, lemon juice, cumin, pepper, garlic, and olive oil in the bowl of a food processor and process until smooth and creamy, about 1 minute.

The spread can be stored in an airtight container in the refrigerator for up to 1 week.

SALTED CARAMEL SAUCE

Makes about 1½ cups

How can something so simple be so good? Salted caramel sauce is just sugar, cream, salt, and your loving time. You will be tempted to lick the spoon, but wait until the sauce is just warm to the touch. Drizzle it over ice cream or use it for the Caramel Cake (page 160).

¾ cup heavy cream	1 cup granulated sugar	¼ teaspoon flaky sea salt, such as Jacobsen or Maldon

Pull the cream out of the refrigerator an hour or so in advance to come up to room temperature. Or heat it in a microwave-safe bowl for 30-second intervals until it is at room temperature, a minute or so. Set aside.

Put 2 tablespoons of the sugar in a heavy nonreactive saucepan and set over medium heat. Watch closely as the sugar melts around the edges and starts to turn a beautiful amber color: you are making caramel. Stir the sugar with a heat-resistant spoon, then add another 2 tablespoons sugar and cook it in the same way. Continue to add the rest of the sugar 2 tablespoons at a time, waiting for it to be completely melted each time before adding more and stirring frequently as it melts and the color deepens. Do not walk away even for a second—the sugar can go from golden caramel to burnt in a flash.

When the caramel is a deep mahogany color, remove the pan from the heat and immediately, but slowly, pour in the cream. (If the cream is cold, the caramel will seize up and you may get some lumps of hardened caramel, but if this happens, there is no need to panic—just return the pan to the stove and stir over low heat until the caramel is completely melted and smooth.) Stir in the sea salt and let cool.

The sauce can be stored in an airtight container in the refrigerator for up to 2 weeks. When you are ready to use it, place the container in a large bowl of hot water and gently stir until it warms up and is ready to drizzle.

Tip: At the bakery, we invest in pure sea salts to give the final flourish to some of our baked goods and savory dishes too. One of our favorites, Jacobsen Salt Co. sea salt, is hand-harvested off the Oregon coast. The salt is flaky and delicious, and a small pinch makes a world of difference for brownies, cookies, popcorn, and, of course, the salted caramel sauce.

CHOCOLATE HONEY FUDGE SAUCE

Makes 2 cups

Many commercial hot fudge sauces are made with corn syrup, but we like to avoid corn syrup when possible, and we've found that it's easy to substitute honey for it in many recipes. Honey brings a lovely sweet note to this fudge sauce; you'll want to make it to pour over your next bowl of vanilla bean ice cream.

⅔ cup heavy cream
½ cup clover honey
⅓ cup packed light brown sugar

¼ cup Dutch-processed cocoa powder
1 cup bittersweet chocolate chips

2 tablespoons unsalted butter, cut into pieces, at room temperature
4 teaspoons pure vanilla extract
¾ teaspoon fine sea salt

In a small heavy saucepan, combine the cream, honey, sugar, cocoa powder, and half of the chocolate chips, stir together with a heat-resistant spatula, and bring to a boil over medium heat, stirring frequently, then reduce the heat and simmer, stirring frequently, for 3 minutes.

Remove from the heat, add the remaining chocolate chips, the butter, vanilla, and salt, and stir until smooth.

Let the sauce cool slightly, stirring occasionally, and use immediately. Or cool completely, pour into a jar, cover, and refrigerate for up to 1 month. To serve, warm gently in a saucepan over low heat (or in the microwave oven) before spooning it over the ice cream of your choice.

BEE STING HONEY

Makes about 1½ cups

Spiced honey is one of my favorite condiments. I serve it with cream cheese and crackers, baked brie, and baguettes; I pour it on chicken wings to give them a kick. Follow the amounts exactly to make a pleasantly spicy honey, or increase the cayenne to make it as hot as you like. Be sure to use your favorite local honey too. We get ours from our friend Brandon's folks' farm in Tylertown, Mississippi.

1 cup honey

¼ cup cider vinegar

¼ teaspoon cayenne pepper

½ teaspoon red pepper flakes

¼ teaspoon fine sea salt

In a medium nonreactive saucepan, combine the honey, vinegar, cayenne, red pepper flakes, and salt and bring to a boil over medium heat. Reduce the heat to low and simmer for 5 minutes. Remove from the heat and let cool to room temperature.

The honey can be stored in an airtight container in the refrigerator for up to 1 month.

HOMEMADE SYRUPS

When we say we make everything at the bakery by hand, we are not kidding: we even make the syrups for our drinks.

If you read the labels on the stuff that stocks the shelves of most grocery stores and coffee shops, it may surprise and even shock you. So I make syrups myself, which allows me to have control over the ingredients that are used. There is no need for syrup with mystery ingredients—thank you very much! You can be as creative as you like, and once you start making your own syrups, trust me, you will think of all kinds of flavor combinations.

These handcrafted syrups make our signature drinks at our coffee counter extra special. At home, they can give a special flair to your morning routine.

You can use syrups for everything from topping pancakes, French toast, and waffles to flavoring cakes. Or use them to make refreshing mocktails (see the Sweet Note on page 292).

VANILLA SYRUP
Makes 2½ cups

2 cups water
2 cups granulated sugar
2 vanilla beans, split lengthwise

In a medium heavy saucepan, combine the water and sugar and bring to a boil over medium-high heat, stirring to dissolve the sugar. Reduce the heat to medium-low, add the vanilla beans, and simmer for 5 minutes, stirring occasionally to ensure that the bottom of the pan doesn't scorch. Remove from the heat and let cool to room temperature.

Remove the vanilla beans and pour the cooled syrup into a jar with a lid. Add the vanilla beans and cover tightly. The syrup can be refrigerated for up to 1 month.

BOURBON SORGHUM SYRUP

Makes 1½ cups

1½ cups packed light brown sugar
1¼ cups water
3 tablespoons sorghum
3 tablespoons Kentucky bourbon
½ teaspoon pure vanilla extract
Pinch of fine sea salt

In a medium heavy saucepan, combine the brown sugar and water and bring to a boil over medium-high heat, stirring to dissolve the sugar. Reduce the heat to medium-low, add the sorghum, bourbon, vanilla, and salt, and simmer for 5 minutes, stirring occasionally so the bottom of the pan doesn't scorch. Remove from the heat and let cool to room temperature.

Pour the cooled syrup into a jar and cover tightly with a lid. The syrup can be refrigerated for up to 1 month.

HONEY LAVENDER SYRUP

Try this syrup in sweet iced tea.
Makes 2½ cups

2 cups water
2 cups granulated sugar
2 tablespoons wildflower honey
2 tablespoons food-grade dried lavender (see Resources, page 293)
4 green cardamom pods, crushed

In a medium heavy saucepan, combine the water, sugar, and honey and bring to a boil over medium-high heat, stirring to dissolve the sugar. Reduce the heat to medium-low, add the lavender and cardamom, and simmer for 5 minutes, stirring occasionally so the bottom of the pan doesn't scorch. Remove from the heat and let cool to room temperature.

Set a fine-mesh sieve over a bowl and pour the syrup through the sieve; discard the lavender and cardamom. Pour the syrup into a jar with a lid and cover tightly. The syrup can be refrigerated for up to 1 month.

HAZELNUT SYRUP

Makes 1¼ cups

1 cup water
1 cup granulated sugar
½ cup hazelnuts, roughly chopped

In a medium heavy saucepan, combine the water and sugar and bring to a boil over medium-high heat, stirring to dissolve the sugar. Reduce the heat to medium-low, add the hazelnuts, and simmer for 5 minutes, stirring occasionally so the bottom of the pan doesn't scorch. Remove from the heat and let cool to room temperature.

Place a fine-mesh sieve over a bowl and pour the syrup through the sieve; discard the hazelnuts. Pour the syrup into a jar with a lid and cover tightly. The syrup can be refrigerated for up to 1 month.

CHOCOLATE SYRUP

Makes 2 cups

1 cup unsweetened cocoa powder
1 cup granulated sugar
1 cup water
½ teaspoon fine sea salt
1 tablespoon pure vanilla extract

In a medium bowl, whisk together the cocoa powder and sugar.

In a medium heavy saucepan, combine the water, salt, and vanilla and stir to combine. Add the cocoa-sugar mixture, whisking to combine. Bring to a low boil over medium-low heat, stirring to dissolve the sugar, then boil for 2 minutes, stirring occasionally so the bottom of the pan doesn't scorch. The mixture will thicken just slightly, but it will thicken into a syrup-like consistency as it cools. Remove from the heat and let cool to room temperature.

Pour the cooled syrup into a jar with a lid and cover tightly. The syrup can be refrigerated for up to 1 month.

GINGERSNAP SYRUP

We love to add this syrup to a glass of seltzer over ice with a sprig of mint to create a light, refreshing summery drink. It has become one of the most popular syrups we make at the bakery—many of our customers request it in their lattes.

Makes about 3½ cups

4 cups granulated sugar
3 cups water
½ pound ginger, scrubbed and thinly sliced
1 cinnamon stick
4 green cardamom pods, crushed

In a medium heavy saucepan, combine the sugar, water, ginger, cinnamon stick, and cardamom pods and bring to a boil over medium heat, stirring to dissolve the sugar. Reduce the heat and simmer gently for 30 minutes. Remove from the heat and let cool to room temperature.

Set a fine-mesh sieve over a bowl and pour the syrup through the sieve. Put the cinnamon stick in a jar and discard the ginger and cardamom. Pour the syrup into the jar and cover tightly. The syrup can be refrigerated for up to 1 month.

BLACKBERRY SYRUP

Use this syrup to create a refreshing mocktail the entire family can enjoy; see the Sweet Note on page 292. Of course, you can use it to make an adult beverage too. I can't resist blackberries, but you can use any fruit you like and even mix fruits too. Try strawberries, raspberries, peaches, rhubarb, or cherries.

Makes about 2 cups

1 cup granulated sugar
1 cup water
1½ cups fresh or frozen blackberries

Combine the sugar, water, and blackberries in a medium saucepan and bring to a boil over high heat, stirring to dissolve the sugar. Turn the heat down to low and simmer, stirring occasionally, until the fruit is very soft, 20 to 25 minutes.

Remove from the heat and pour through a fine-mesh strainer set over a bowl. Press on the fruit with a wooden spoon to release all the syrup. Let cool to room temperature.

Pour the syrup into a jar with a lid and cover tightly. The syrup can be refrigerated for up to 2 weeks.

HOW TO MAKE A MOCKTAIL

What's a mocktail, you ask? It's a nonalcoholic beverage that has something sparkly in it, like seltzer, club soda, ginger ale, or even ginger beer, and some homemade syrup too. We served mocktails at our first Saturday Supper Club hosted at the bakery, and our nondrinking friends swooned. Stock your next party bar with a variety of homemade syrups and mixers so that folks can create their own blends.

Our mocktails take some cues from cocktail culture, so before you make one, fill a small bowl with colored sanding sugar and lightly dampen the rim of your drinking glass with the juice from a lemon wedge (or water). Dip the rim of the glass in the sugar; it adds a bit of whimsy and some color too. Add flavor and fragrance to your drink with the addition of fresh fruit or sprigs of herbs such as lavender, mint, or basil. You can also make fancy ice cubes by filling an ice tray with fresh fruit and sparkling water. Put a few cubes in each glass before serving.

BLACKBERRY LIME SPRITZER *Makes 1*

3 tablespoons Blackberry Syrup (page 291)
Juice of 1 lime
12 ounces seltzer water

Place a few ice cubes in a tall drinking glass. Fill the glass with the syrup and lime juice. Pour the seltzer over top. Pop in a straw, give it a stir, and enjoy!

HONEY LAVENDER LEMONADE COOLER *Makes 1*

5 tablespoons Honey Lavender Syrup (page 288)
Juice of 1 lemon
12 ounces seltzer water
Slice of fresh lemon for garnish

Place a few ice cubes in a tall drinking glass. Fill the glass with the syrup and lemon juice. Pour the seltzer over top. Give it a stir, garnish with the slice of lemon, and enjoy!

ISLAND BREEZE FIZZY *Makes 1*

3 tablespoons Gingersnap Syrup (page 290)
3 tablespoons pineapple juice
12 ounces seltzer water

Place a few ice cubes in a tall drinking glass. Fill the glass with the syrup and pineapple juice. Pour the seltzer over top. Stir and enjoy.

RESOURCES

We have included in this list some of our absolute favorite places in Savannah and on-line. If you visit any of our local Savannah shops, be sure to tell them that we sent you!

Anson Mills
www.ansonmills.com
An artisanal mill in South Carolina that hand-mills grits, rice, cornmeal, and specialty flours from organic heirloom grains.

Anthropologie
www.anthropologie.com
I love their vintage-inspired home goods like the copper measuring cups, beautiful hand-painted measuring spoons, bakeware, and whisks.

Bake It Pretty
www.bakeitpretty.com
A fantastic online shop that stocks nostalgic supplies for baking, crafting, party making, and everyday celebrating.

Bell'occhio
www.bellochio.com
A wonderland filled with treasures and charm. I love to use the blackboard oil cloth to write my menu displays and the filet mignon string bag to take to the farmers' market. Bonus—all purchases are gift-wrapped in their signature snappy wrapping.

Cup to Cup Coffee Roasters
www.cuptocupcoffee.com
We source our special blend of coffee from a local small-batch roaster located in Savannah. The perfect accompaniment to all of our sweet treats, it is hand-delivered to us by the owner, James Spano, himself.

Emily Isabella
www.emilyisabella.bigcartel.com
We love Emily's note cards and tea towels—especially the one inspired by her favorite bakers. You will find Emily's beautiful illustrations throughout this book.

Etsy
www.etsy.com
An online community of artisans buying and selling handcrafted and vintage items.

Everyday Is a Holiday
www.everyday-is-a-holiday.blogspot.com
Art inspired by baked goods and vintage treasures? Yes, please! We adore our sign from them, which says, "Keep calm and have a cupcake."

Fishs Eddy
www.fishseddy.com
Vintage dishes, glasses and serveware, kitchen linens, and so much more. It's a treasure trove of everything I love all in one place.

Hedley & Bennett
www.hedleyandbennett.com
Our absolute favorite source for cooking aprons. They are made in the U.S.A., and they are good-looking too. We wear them loud and proud.

Herriott Grace
www.herriottgrace.com
A supplier of hand-carved and hand-turned wooden objects, including rolling pins, cake pedestals, spoons, and serving boards, as well as kitchen linens, cake flags, and cookie cutters.

Katie Runnels
www.theconstantgatherer.blogspot.com
Vintage treasures, including my collection of cupcake toppers. Katie, a mixed-media artist, says she is inspired by her love of family traditions, vintage wares, and my buttercream frosting.

King Arthur Flour Baker's Catalogue
www.kingarthurflour.com
An employee-owned company that has been making pure flours (including almond flour) for more than two hundred years and is an essential source for baking supplies.

Layer Cake Shop
www.layercakeshop.com
A one-stop shop for adding vintage charm to homemade cookies, cakes, and cupcakes. You will find cookie cutters, meringue powder, luster dust, colored sanding sugar, and many other things to allow you to be creative in the kitchen.

Measure: A Fabric Parlor
www.etsy.com/shop/measureafabricparlor
One of my favorite shops, filled with beautiful fabric and notions for crafting projects.

The Paris Market
www.theparismarket.com
Located in the heart of Savannah's historic district, the Paris Market is a beautiful storehouse of treasures, filled with visual eye candy. They stock many of our treats in their café.

Prospector Co.
www.prospectorco.com
One of the coolest stores in Savannah, this is a thoughtfully merchandised shop that carries many of my favorite things, from kitchen soaps to candles to home decor.

Rycraft
www.cookiestamp.com
Their finely detailed terra-cotta cookie stamps are handcrafted in the U.S.A.

Shop Sweet Lulu
www.shopsweetlulu.com
Lovely food packaging and party-styling essentials sourced from all over the world. The magic is in the details, so shop here to pick up some floral fiesta pom-pom picks and pretty paper straws.

Signe Sugar
www.etsy.com/shop/signesugar
Create the cake of your dreams using pieces from this lovely collection of cake decorations handmade by Sarah Donato. She believes a cake should always be a beautiful gift and should make you smile, and we agree!

Sucre Shop
www.sucreshop.com
The colorful hand-printed wooden utensils and plates are not only eco-friendly but just the perfect touch for setting the table for a dinner party or holiday celebration.

Tiny Things Are Cute
www.tinythingsarecute.com
You'll find many tiny things here, for making Cupcake Surprise Balls (see page 262), as well as cupcake flags, vintage gumball trinkets, and party favors.

West Elm
www.westelm.com
A great source for cooks' tools and bakeware. We especially love their collaborations with handcraftspeople from all over the world.

ACKNOWLEDGMENTS

Griff and I always dreamed of being surrounded by great folks to collaborate with and to share our craft of living a handmade life every day. This book holds the key to our hearts and shares our love of feeding people more than ever.

We would like to thank all of our incredible and talented employees, past and present, from Sugarnauts to bakers to lunch masters, for helping us make meaningful connections every day. We would not have been able to fill the pages of this book without the contributions of our amazing team and so many wonderful friends who gave it a loving touch.

We would like to thank Judy Pray, our editor. She truly gets us and completes us. She is always thinking about how to make us better. We thank her for understanding our crazy schedule and for giving us the support and encouragement to be ourselves while keeping our readers leaning in to our story. It was her enthusiasm and dedication to us that turned two bakers into cookbook authors.

We would like to thank Ann Bramson for always believing that we have something special to share. We especially appreciate her sweet notes, beautiful smile, and warm hugs.

Thank you to the whole Artisan team—Michelle Ishay-Cohen, Sibylle Kazeroid, Jenny Mandel, Allison McGeehon, Nancy Murray, Lia Ronnen, and Judith Sutton—for the tools and encouragement to make it happen.

This book came to life visually thanks to the creative teamwork of our band of soul sisters, Angie Mosier, Lizzie Johnston, and Haylie Waring, who made the very long days of baking and shooting photos one of the best experiences of our lives. Time flies when you are having fun!

When the incomparable photographer Angie Mosier and her amazing assistant, Lizzie Johnston, showed up at the bakery with a big box of vintage accoutrements to share, we knew that magic was about to happen. Thanks to them for sharing their special gifts and the light that follows them both around. Angie and Lizzie made every plate we delivered on set exceed our expectations in the photos. Their talent is awe-inspiring, and it makes us want to eat every page of this book. We appreciate the time and care that they took to make sure that our story was being told visually, and for including our personal treasures that share a part of us in every shot.

Thank you to our dear, sweet friend Haylie Waring for bringing her talent and creativity to this book once again, for her incredible styling, and for producing the MIYs. No one knows our vision better than Haylie does, and she found and foraged all the loving details in the photos on these pages. We ♥ Haylie forever and ever.

Thanks to Halligan Norris Smith for setting up the MIY production studio in her home and for bringing her creativity and attention to detail to every project. We are so thankful for her talent and friendship.

Thanks to the incredibly talented Emily Isabella for her beautiful illustrations, which bring the handmade quality to this book in a way no one else ever could have. Thank you, too, for standing beside us even when we were just dreaming of this book. Emily is a treasure and we are so happy to have her in our lives.

Thanks to Paula Deen for always welcoming us with open arms. We ♥ Paula.

Thanks to Diane Kaufman for her guidance and friendship.

Thanks to Grace Bonney and Julia Turshen for their amazing support of everything we do. They are a constant source of inspiration to us.

Thanks to Kiki Tillman for bringing her celebrity style to the building and for letting us borrow our sweetest baby cake model, Harper Tillman.

Thanks to my one-woman glam squad, Lindsay Nix, for always making me feel beautiful. She is one talented lady!

Thanks to our loyal friends Ginger and Brint Waring for always being available to lend a helping hand and for cheering us on and on.

Thanks to India and Shea Roberts for carrying on the tradition of baking from scratch and putting an extra pinch of love into everything they do.

Last, but certainly not least, we would like to thank our loyal customers and everyone who bought our first cookbook. To those who ventured into the bakery, visiting from all over the world with our book in hand, and for the many kind letters that came in the post, we say thank you, and we are humbled to hear that our book has made a difference in your lives. We appreciate your kindness and support.

Dear Griff:

We are one of the great American love stories. Thank you for being my partner in business and in life and for telling me that I make beautiful dough.

xo, Cheryl

Dear Cheryl:

Your passion for life, your smile from within, and your laughter every day have inspired me to be a better person. I'm so grateful we get to bake together every day and to share our passion with others.

xoxo, Griff

INDEX